D1346313

Spinsters of This Parish

Sandra Laslett

Robson Books

First published in Great Britain in 1990 by Robson Books Ltd
Bolsover House, 5–6 Clipstone Street, London W1P 7EB

Copyright © 1990 Sandra Laslett

Illustrations by Francis Scappaticci

British Library Cataloguing in Publication Data
Laslett, Sandra
  Spinsters of this parish.
  I. Title
  823.914 [F]

ISBN 0 86051 661 X

Typeset by Selectmove Ltd, London
Printed in Great Britain by
Butler & Tanner Ltd, Frome & London

IF I HAD A HAMMER (Pete Seeger/Lee Hays) © 1962 Tro
Essex Music Ltd, Suite 2.07, Plaza 535 Kings Road, London
SW10 0SZ. International Copyright Secured. All Rights
Reserved. Used by Permission.

FOR MY HUSBAND, MICHAEL

Contents

Acknowledgements

I wish to express my grateful thanks to the following people: my husband Michael for checking my manuscript; my parents for sending me to church, without which this book could not have been written; and to David and Sheila for their encouragement and enthusiasm.

Foreword

From the age of two, when I was taken screaming into Sunday school, until I was seventeen, by which time I had got used to the idea, my life was synonymous with that of the parish. In this book I describe my ecclesiastical experiences and observations from the late nineteen-fifties and the sixties, and the colourful characters I came across (I have changed all their names – excepting that of Great Aunt Flo!). The Church year rotated with reassuring repetition and revolving with it were the clergy and the Spinsters of this Parish. In the final chapters I view the parochial life of this typical English parish through the eyes of the spinsters themselves, as they each exercise their exceptional talent for creating chaos. I hope that you enjoy reading this book as much as I have enjoyed writing it.

Sunday School

'Morning has broken', we chorused, 'Blackbird has spoken', we squawked – this, decades before it became a popular song – and we thumped our mittened palms together and stomped up and down in our wellingtons on the wooden floor. You could be forgiven for thinking that this was the commencement of the Charismatic Movement; in actual fact it was twenty tiny tots trying to keep warm in a wooden hut on a freezing Sunday in February.

The antiquated electric wall fires positioned at ceiling level were totally ineffective for the purpose for which they were intended. However they were extremely efficient in melting the snow on the tin roof. It was then a simple matter for any heat produced to leave promptly via the roof, thus depriving the infants seated on the floor below of any scrap of warmth at all.

The babies, that is the two- to four-year-olds, methodically recited the Lord's Prayer each week. My rendition being 'Forgive us our Christmases'. Christmases were familiar; trespasses were not. Jesus bade us to shine like candles; we were told to let our light shine and that we were wanted for sunbeams. We would have been useful in any power cut and we probably generated more kilowatts than the wall fires. The freezing conditions were accepted as the cross we had to bear. No doubt today an NSPCC inspector would have been sent post-haste by an irate and distraught parent to investigate such polar conditions. In his wake would follow hoards of eager journalists writing headlines such as 'Tiny tots allowed to freeze in tin hut', and it would have been branded as a lunatic-fringe religion which took 'suffer the little children' too literally. In those days winters were cold and that was that. All that remained was for our mothers to collect us and half drag, half carry us home, plunge us into hot mustard baths and pour boiling Oxo down our throats. We survived – just!

From the infants, we progressed to the junior Sunday school in the church hall. On average there were fifty children present, carefully segregated into male and female classes by the spinsterly Sunday school superintendent. At lesson time one class of boys would disappear into the choir vestry, mission unknown, and their elderly teacher would arrive each week with a small lap dog stuffed into his overcoat.

We sang hymns, gabbled the creed and stuck picture stamps in our stamp books. A miniature altar was erected at one end of the hall, complete with candles, cross and flowers. Behind this presided Miss Peebles, an elderly upright spinster who had previously taught my mother. Each week some poor unfortunate was delegated to read the collect, and for this purpose it benefited one to be fully conversant beforehand as to exactly which Sunday it was. During Trinity one lost count completely, as there are twenty-four Sundays after Trinity. It was equally easy to get lost after Epiphany. Miss Peebles would beam at us all through horn-rimmed spectacles and ask the dreaded question, 'Now children, which Sunday is it this week?' Hands would shoot up. 'Fifth after Epiphany', said one (shot in the dark) 'Fourth', called another (uninspired guess) 'Quinquagesima', shouted some bright spark. 'No dear, that's not for another two weeks; this week it's. . .? Now come on; it's important.' There is silence and she begins to get agitated. 'Well, in that case I'll have to tell you. It's Septuagesima.' We would then have to chant 'Septuagesima, Sexagesima, Quinquagesima' until we were brainwashed with this vital piece of information, which indeed I have never forgotten.

Mostly we sang hymns from torn and faded red hymnals. Very occasionally we ventured on a chorus. We knew only two, one being 'I will make you fishers of men, if you follow me' and this we sang to the accompaniment of a hoarse and highly strung piano. Dumpy Miss Venables, thrilled at being allowed to play a 'goey' number, giving it her all. She let rip with arpeggios and trills and a thundering bass rhythm played fortissimo. Her brown felt hat tipping to one side, her hair flying as she sped up and down the piano, feet thumping the pedals as if treading grapes and her posterior defying the law of gravity as it kept leaving the piano stool to accompany her flight up the keys. Faster and faster she played, faster and faster we sang until she triumphantly crashed down the final chord and fell exhausted on to her chair. The only other chorus we knew was entitled 'He Lives'. Miss Peebles would commence singing this in an extremely high and unlikely key, and the Spotty Youth now in charge of the ivories (Miss Venables being unfit, having expended all her energies) would attempt to accompany her. We joined in, only to stop at a point where the notes soared out of vocal range. Not so Miss Peebles. With her string of amber-coloured glass beads from Woolworth's bouncing on her chest, she was undeterred and would screech 'He lives' at such a high level of decibels that with bated breath we waited for the shattering of a leaded-light window. Unfortunately we were always disappointed.

If it was one's birthday, one had the dubious privilege of being allowed to light the candles on the altar and to choose a bible bookmark. I am ashamed to say that no one opened a bible from one week to the next, and consequently no one could generate much enthusiasm for the markers, but as Miss Peebles joyfully spread them out on the altar top for our perusal we would feel obliged to fake our pleasure. Lighting the candles could be hazardous. If the PCC had known about it they would have increased their insurance policy against fire risk. Miss Peebles would shakily strike a match and the birthday boy or girl would attempt to light a coloured taper from the flame. If several children had birthdays, extra candles would be put on the altar till it resembled a high mass. There would then be a mad rush to light all the tapers before the match burnt Miss Peebles' fingers and went out. The tapers invariably did go out or flared dangerously before the candle could be lit, thereby reducing the birthday boy's chances of seeing another birthday. A good five minutes would be spent in starting the procedure all over again. The safest way (as instructed by Miss Peebles) to extinguish the lighted taper was to give it a quick blow and instantly stuff it unceremoniously into a conveniently placed vase of Michaelmas daisies. With a delightful hiss the hot taper plunged into the cold water and a satisfying spiral of steam and smoke was emitted for the next few moments. Peering shortsightedly through the smoking daisies like a high priest burning incense on a papal altar, Miss Peebles aged visibly as the morning wore on.

On various occasions such as Harvest Festival the vicar would allow us into the church – not to stay, but merely to pass through. We handed over our harvest gifts as we were hustled up the chancel. On this particular Sunday in the Church calendar we would all arrive early at the church hall, clutching our harvest gifts. The usual gift consisted of a cardboard box with the front cut away, and into this was piled a variety of produce. Mine usually consisted of large Bramley apples, choice carrots, tender sticks of rhubarb, large home-grown, greenhouse tomatoes, runner beans and the ubiquitous bunch of Michaelmas daisies. A few children had been sent with packets of cornflakes which had probably been whipped out of the store-cupboard without much forethought and were indicative of the coming age when people would regard food as something which came in tins and consisted largely of 'E numbers'. My early training of what constituted a healthy harvest has stood me in good stead ever since. Other children, with ostentatious parents, arrived carrying enormous cardboard boxes piled high with oranges, bananas, pineapples, and other tropical fruits.

Miss Peebles would instruct us to put our harvest gifts in a safe place until such time as we were summonsed to the church. Miss Peebles' love of Michaelmas daisies was even more evident on Harvest Sunday. Extra vases were arranged on the altar and on the window sills. 'Now our first hymn this morning wil be . . .', began Miss Peebles, but we had all beaten her to it and had already turned in our hymn-books to 'We plough the fields and scatter'. It was the same routine each year without fail. Miss Peebles warbled on about soft refreshing rain, while Miss Venables ploughed enthusiastically with her piano pedals and scattered notes in all directions. At the end of the hymn we all sat down and Miss Peebles told us about Ruth who went gleaning in the fields. The boys got this mixed up with scrumping and thought that this hitherto illegal practice now had the blessing of the Church. Miss Peebles also told us all she knew about farmers sowing seeds and growing crops, which wasn't very much. It was not in the least bit interesting and one little five-year-old decided to relieve the boredom by making a start on a bunch of bananas from his harvest box. It wasn't long before others were fighting the temptation to eat just one of the rosy apples from their harvest gifts. Fortunately at that moment Mr Bulmer, one of the churchwardens, arrived and announced we were wanted in the church in five minutes.

'Find a partner,' twittered Miss Peebles, making it sound as if we were about to do a harvest dance. The couples then formed a long line, each child hidden behind a mountain of produce. Inevitably someone would drop a bunch of grapes or the bottom of a box would fall out altogether under the weight of the harvest and Miss Peebles would then have to mop up the floor while Miss Venables mopped up the tears. Once order had been restored we would begin to process through the passages to the church. One year, a boy mysteriously burst his packet of cornflakes (we suspected a deliberate act of sabotage) and the ensuing mess of crushed cornflakes all the way up the steps did nothing to endear us to the vicar.

Palm Sunday was another annual event which was eagerly awaited. Miss Peebles would instruct us on the correct way to receive our palm crosses from the vicar. Each year she instructed the boys not to turn the crosses upside down and use them as swords. Each year they dared each other to incur Miss Peebles' wrath and turned the crosses upside down and engaged in dramatic sword fights. We would form a crocodile and thread our way through the maze of concrete stairways and dim stone corridors that separated the lambs in the hall from the sheep in the church. The vicar believed in separate pens; he couldn't cope with all his flock at once. We would feel highly privileged and blessed if we received our crosses from the vicar himself, satisfied if they were given to us by the curate, rather hard done by if it was our misfortune to be given them by an altar server and downright deprived if they were handed over by a grinning choirboy, attired in grubby surplice, who had only recently graduated from Sunday school.

Back in the hall, Miss Peebles would hand round the collection bag, and pennies and halfpennies would roll around the floor before the bag was finally deposited among the conglomeration of objects already on the altar.

Miss Peebles remained completely unruffled most of the time – but once we were treated to another side of her nature. The majority of children were extremely well behaved (it was in the days before free expression was encouraged) and we were a silent bunch. That is with the exception of Roger and Stephen, two brothers who found that being still and silent was totally beyond their capabilities. On one particular Sunday they had been told repeatedly by Miss Peebles to put their fire engine away. She had been terribly nice about it, but after Stephen had sent the fire engine racing down the hall and it had crashed violently into the altar, Miss Peebles exploded. She stormed over to their class and started to shout hysterically. Grabbing them by the necks of their jumpers she frog-marched them to the door shouting, 'I will not have it, get out and stay out!' She dumped them outside and shut the door behind them. As she walked back to the altar she was shaking visibly and so were we. The mild-mannered Miss Peebles had undergone a complete metamorphosis in front of our eyes and it was extremely worrying. It had worried us and upset Miss Peebles but it had been a complete embarrassment to Miss Venables – Roger and Stephen were her nephews.

The hands on the clock stood at ten past eleven precisely. At ten past eleven precisely each week Miss Peebles would intone the benediction, and at the final 'Amen' we pulled on our coats, threw our hymn-books into the cupboard and joined the scrum fighting and jostling its way through the door. To impassioned pleas of 'Children, please don't leave the cupboard so untidy' we fled, leaving Miss Peebles to contemplate next week's lesson and the wisdom of retiring before it was too late.

The Church Bazaar

The Church bazaar held annually in November was an 'essential' part of the Church calendar, falling as it did between Michaelmas and Christmas. Each year was the same. . . husbands, who usually only attended christenings, weddings and funerals, had the added burden of having to attend the 'Putting up of the stalls on a Friday night' ceremony as well.

Early Saturday morning the good ladies would arrive, clutching tins, bags and their sandwiches, it being an all-day event. Soon, crêpe paper and tinsel abounded on every stall. All the ladies wore aprons although the necessity of this whilst selling knitted dishcloths and Christmas wrapping paper, somewhat eluded me.

The white elephant stall on the stage overflowed with the left-overs from the recent jumble sale, sending a river of dog-eared *Reader's Digest*s cascading down the steps, threatening to engulf an old retainer precariously seated at a whist-drive table, who was courageously selling jars of pickled beetroot.

The vicar would beam genially at everyone and buy the odd dishcloth and lavender bag for Mrs vicar and have the odd go on this and that, usually retreating to the kitchen after his tiring duties for a free cup of tea. There were the usual stalls full of crocheted 'thingamies' and knitted 'what nots', along with enough peg bags to supply every lady in the church twice over.

The bottle stall always did quite well with a chance to win anything from tomato ketchup and Vim to a bottle of 'affaire de coeur' perfume – originally an unwanted gift, the spinsterly donor feeling it wasn't quite *the* thing! More than once, my mother won back the item she had donated, in the end giving it up as a lost cause.

The Mothers' Union always 'did the teas'. Each year they started the day complaining of the cold, as the ancient radiators ineffectively hiccuped hot water round the cavernous building, losing their heat without any trouble through the open doors, and competing with the wind and rain which was usually trying to come in. By four o'clock most of the ladies had headaches due to the overwhelming fug which had developed during the day. Closely packed bodies in damp raincoats fought their way between stalls, doggedly clutching their 'unwanted gift' prizes and the little something to stuff into Aunt Maud's stocking at Christmas. The odour of warm bodies and damp clothes mingling with the sausage rolls and soup produced a most unsavoury atmosphere but, as no one knew where the pole was that opened the fanlights, the ladies just had to soldier on.

At the far end of the hall resided the cake stall. My mother would buy some of her friend's cakes and the friend would purchase some of my mother's cakes, because, as they both said, 'You *know* where they've *been!*' Anything else on the stall was decidedly suspect.

Then of course there was the 'guess the weight of the cake', 'guess the name of the doll', 'guess the number of beans in the jar', 'guess what the vicar had for dinner last Tuesday week'. The trouble was that no one really wanted to win the cake after the entire congregation had breathed heavily over it while deliberating the weight of its contents of sultanas and concrete icing (it was before the days of cling film, you understand). The doll wasn't in much demand either, having been fitted out for the occasion in woolly garments made from the wool which had been left over after making the knitted 'what nots'; and you had to be pretty desperate to want the haricot beans – still, I wonder what the vicar *did* have for dinner last Tuesday . . .!

If you parted with a threepenny bit, you could immerse yourself up to the armpits in sawdust and have a 'lucky dip.' Not that it was ever that lucky, usually it was something plastic and useless with Hong Kong stamped on the bottom. This could be, and usually was, donated back to the bran tub at the time of the summer fête for some other unsuspecting individual to pull out, only to return it to the Christmas Bazaar. I expect things had been circulating for years.

Towards the end of the afternoon, a voice would announce, 'Now the moment you've all been waiting for, we are going to draw the raffle tickets.' It always went something like this . . .

There would be a general shuffling as people try to locate their tickets. Ladies sift through handbags and aprons for lost tickets, which are finally located behind the tea urn or found after the draw, crumpled up in the rubbish bin along with the wrappings from the digestives and Butter Osbornes. Choirboys barge madly round the hall, trying to drum up last minute business with the raffle books. Then an awed hush falls over those assembled. 'Vicar, perhaps you would care to draw the first ticket,' says the churchwarden. The vicar shortsightedly stabs his hand into the unsold tea cosy now doing duty holding the draw tickets and pulls out 'Pink ticket, number one-hundred-and-thirty-eight'. 'Fix!' shouts someone as the curate stumps forward and selects the bottle of gin from the prizes table. The churchwarden then asks a Mothers' Union member to draw a ticket.

'Green ticket, number two-hundred-and-forty-two', he calls. Everyone looks down, 'Oh, missed it by one' (surprising how many miss it by one) and 'if that had been yellow/blue/pink I would have won' (ditto). 'Green ticket, number two-hundred-and-forty-two', bellows the churchwarden again, looking distinctly agitated as no one comes forward to claim the prize. It seems that number two-four-two has gone home and not left his address – can't say I blame him . . .

Evensong

The sonorous sound of the church bell chimed six times and then stopped. 'Service starts in fifteen minutes,' it warned. My mother and I were half-way up the hill. As we reached the top and turned the corner, the bell rang out again; its warning this time, 'Ten minutes to go and you'd better hurry.' On reaching the church door it rang out a final six times, saying, 'If you're not here now, you're going to be late.'

My mother and I entered the church and sat down at the back, at the end of a pew. The church was not exactly full, although anyone peering through the door could have formed that impression. Actually, little old ladies had whole pews to themselves, whilst others in the back two rows were crammed together like peas in a pod. The reason? On the right we had the Claustrophobics' Club and on the left we had Agoraphobics Anonymous. We all felt relatively safe at the back near the door, although the coveted end pews were sometimes fought over. The weapons used were no more than determined looks, but they could have the effect of a cannonball and people would reluctantly shuffle up to make room. If it didn't work, the loser would have to squeeze himself between several pairs of feet and the pew, taking care not to trip over a hassock and disturb the peace.

It was a select few that attended evensong. It had an air of tranquillity about it, although some may have thought senility when looking round the congregation. The curate moved about softly in the chancel and the organ murmured sweet nothings to itself. Pools of yellow light lit up parts of the church and threw others into deep shadow. My mother gave me a sharp dig with her elbow. Following her gaze I spotted Miss Birch who had somehow managed to come in quietly and was sitting on the other side of the aisle. We all sat bolt upright each wearing an expression suitable for the occasion. The rustling of plastic macs (it was invariably raining) heralded the arrival of Miss Peebles, closely followed by Miss Venables. Miss Peebles made her way to the pew a few rows in front of us. She proceeded to wipe the raindrops from her glasses with a lace-edged handkerchief and then with a loud click she shut her handbag, the noise echoing out of all proportion round the pews. Miss Venables plonked herself down next to Miss Peebles, twittering in a distressed fashion. It soon became evident that Miss Venables had mislaid her reading glasses without which her prayer book would be useless. They opened Miss Peebles's handbag to see if the glasses had inadvertently found their way in there; but no, they could not be found and the handbag was closed with another resounding click. As an aside my mother whispered, 'I expect they've been to tea with each other.' By now Miss Venables was rifling through her raincoat pockets. The organ music had ceased and we awaited the appearance of the vicar. Miss Venables' search did not appear to have borne any fruit.

With a whisper of vestments the vicar emerged from the sanctuary. He started by saying, 'We will begin our worship this evening by singing hymn number one-hundred-and-forty-four.' Partially deaf old ladies, who were unable to quite catch what he said, looked up at the hymn-boards for confirmation, but were faced with a dilemma. There were two hymn-boards, one positioned over the pulpit, the other over the lectern. Unfortunately one set was correct, while the other board still displayed the numbers for the morning's worship. So the old ladies gamely took pot luck and this was how some of the congregation came to be singing 'New Every Morning is the Love' while the rest sang 'The Day Thou Gavest Lord is Ended'. Half-way through, the organist got carried away and pulled out all the stops, drowning us all. The vicar appeared not to notice. During the hymn Miss Venables had been unable to sing as she was busily emptying the contents of her handbag on to a hassock. This time she had been successful in locating the errant spectacles and had returned all the items to her handbag by the time we came to the end of the hymn. There followed a few seconds of complete silence. Unfortunately, Miss Venables chose that precise moment to drop her spectacle case on the floor. All eyes turned in her direction. Miss Peebles stared straight ahead and tried to pretend that she had nothing to do with Miss Venables. The moment was quickly over as it became evident that there was another distraction. The electric light over the lectern appeared not to be working and it was obvious that the vicar was somewhat nonplussed. It was not done to read from anywhere else, so we had to wait while the curate and a sidesman exchanged the bulb with the one from the pulpit.

The reading over, the curate whipped out the lectern light and replaced it in the pulpit in time for the sermon. In the meantime we sang a psalm, during which Miss Venables dropped her prayer book, and then we sat in silence and listened to the sermon. I say silence, but this was not strictly accurate, for it suddenly seemed that most of the congregation had developed consumption or, at best, bronchitis. Throats were cleared long and loud. Some were shaken by paroxysms of coughing. Coughing it seemed was infectious and no one liked to be left out. I nearly had a choking fit as I tried to stifle a giggle when I saw Miss Peebles pop a large peppermint humbug into her mouth and surreptitiously pass one to Miss Venables. Both old ladies finished out the sermon with jaws working overtime as they attempted to finish their humbugs before they had to sing again.

We sang the Magnificat and watched the candles flickering in the insidious draughts. The vicar glided silently about the chancel as if floating on an unseen ethereal current. He seemed to maintain a total detachment from his distant parishioners who were clustered in the deep gloom in the nether regions of the church. Exactly what he was doing up at the altar remained a mystery. However, after concluding his devotional ministrations he would proceed to the chancel steps and raise his hand in a final blessing.

The organ played softly, acting like a lullaby on the two old boys who had nodded off to sleep during the vicar's soporific sermon. Miss Peebles had been using her hassock as a foot rest and this had obviously relaxed her as she lifted a gloved hand to stifle a yawn. Miss Venables sat quite still with a dreamy expression on her face.

Suddenly, without warning the organ loudly crashed a final discordant note and the music ceased. The organist was cold and tired and he wanted to go home for his supper. The loud chord had achieved its desired effect and the old boys woke with a start and Miss Venables was forced back to planet earth with a bump. Miss Peebles took it as a cue to gather together their paraphernalia that had collected in the pew. Miss Venables rescued the plastic rainhats which had been left to dry on a pew end.

The vicar stood by the door murmuring platitudes to his flock as they passed out into the night. Two efficient sidesmen snatched prayer books from parishioners as they gathered round the door. In the porch was an umbrella stand containing a curious collection of umbrellas waiting for their owners. It was possible to identify which umbrella belonged to whom. The curate's was voluminous and black. Miss Peebles' was navy-blue and serviceable. Miss Birch's had an immense handle, and the multi-coloured golfing umbrella belonged to the Major, a military gentleman of the First World War who was now in charge of hymn-books. The umbrella with all the spokes sticking out belonged to the vicar and the lilac one with a fussy tassel had to belong to Miss Venables. Miss Birch bade us all a hearty goodnight in her deep, gruff voice and then she strode manfully into the darkness. Outside, we said goodbye to Miss Peebles who appeared to be having trouble with her dentures as she spoke. No doubt the humbug still adhered in some to some inaccessible part of her plate. We would have said goodnight to Miss Venables but she was otherwise engaged; her umbrella had just blown inside out and was behaving like a sail in the strong wind, propelling her at a fast rate of knots into the blackness. The handbag, gloves and scarf she had been carrying scattered along the path at intervals, snatched from her grasp by the wind during her heroic attempt to keep up with the umbrella. Miss Peebles mumbled, somewhat inarticulately through the humbug remains, 'What a night!' although it sounded as if she muttered 'What a sight!' and as at that precise moment Miss Venables and her plastic rainhat chose to part company, I rather think that is what she did say.

The Church Parade

Miss Hilary Birch, dressed in her Guide uniform with her captain's hat perched at a jaunty angle, marched briskly up the hill to the church. The first Sunday in the month was church parade Sunday. The Scout band assembled outside the church and a motley collection of Guides and Cubs waited to be told to 'fall in'. As Brownies we were never allowed to march behind the band and it seemed the height of injustice. 'Why', we asked, 'are the Cubs allowed to march and we are not?' Brown Owl would just nod wisely and, with an adult's skill of avoiding a question, she would push us into the church. I expect today's Brownies have burnt their pixie badges, donned woggles and now march with the best of 'em. 'Fall in and don't forget to start off on the left foot,' barked Miss Birch. In rows of four abreast the Guides shuffled in behind the Scouts; tiny Cubs tagged on behind. 'Forward march!' shouted the scoutmaster and off we set.

Our route took us through various roads in the parish. The booming of the bass drum reverberated back and forth between the houses. Keeping the bass drum company were a dozen side drums. These Scouts did twiddly things with their drum sticks and at times appeared to stick them up their noses. A very tall Scout played a newly acquired glockenspiel and its fairy chimes tinkled prettily above the booming. The bugles' resonant tones pierced our ear drums. Whole families would gather at their gates and point and wave and generally put us out of step. Others would bang their windows shut and close their doors and their ears to the din.

It was relatively simple to get out of step but extremely difficult to get in again. While everyone else was left–right, left–right, the out of step individual would be right–left, right–left and would then have to execute a nifty skip to change feet. Sometimes this worked, more often it didn't. One could normally put one's feet right by Miss Birch who marched along on the outside. Her beady eye kept a watch for trouble in the ranks. She also kept a watchful eye on the traffic, although she needn't have worried; it kept a wide berth of Miss Birch. After a while we came to the main road and the traffic lights. The lights were red so we marched on the spot. The bugles' strident tones vying with car horns which were pressed long and hard by drivers who were stuck way behind us. The lights then turned to green and the march recommenced. The mace-bearer at the front wheeled sharp left, indicating his direction by an outstretched mace, only just missing an unsuspecting bystander.

The Scouts followed, bass drum booming. The first two rows of Guides also followed. Suddenly the lights turned amber. Miss Birch looked worried and started to accelerate but to no avail; our way was barred by another red light. To our dismay we saw the band march off into the distance and soon they had completely disappeared over the brow of the hill; the bugles and the drum beats became fainter and fainter accompanied by a muted boom–boom.

Eventually the lights changed to green and Miss Birch, narrowly missing a policeman on a bicycle, set off at speed and the rest of us followed at a run. Looking over our shoulders we could see the lights change again and a few tearful Cubs were left standing in the road. The policeman dismounted and kindly escorted them to the pavement. Meanwhile we followed the distant drum beats. Helpful passers-by pointed into the distance and shouted, 'They went that way!' and we hurried on. Puffing triumphantly,

Miss Birch caught up with the band and we all resumed our dignity. Dignity was difficult to keep on windy days when a sudden gust of wind could sweep one's hat off. Often a Guide would break ranks and chase an errant hat along the pavement. A hat, you understand, was never quite the same once it had been flattened by a bus. Miss Birch's cap was well stapled to her head by hair pins and it *never* left its position.

Exhausted, we arrived back at the church in time for the service. Once inside the church Miss Birch dashed round with the collection bags. On church parade Sundays it was the custom for the offering to be collected by the Guides and Scouts. It was a job to be avoided at all costs and our hearts thumped with fear as Miss Birch advanced with the shabby, blue velvet collection bags. We all stared intently at the wooden floor, avoiding the searching gaze of Miss Birch. This was one of the few times when it was beneficial to be seated behind one of the thick, stone pillars, because it afforded excellent cover. Miss Birch always picked a Guide who was smartly turned out to take round the collection bag. We all arrived looking very clean and smart in case we were asked to carry one of the flags but we now set about making ourselves look as disreputable as possible with as much speed as we could. We pulled off our hats and jammed them into the back of the pew in front along with our hymn-books. We undid the buttons on our blouse pockets and loosened the ties around our necks. Miss Birch, who a few moments previously had been most proud of her Guide company, now looked amazed at our changed appearance. She would seize upon two of the least dishevelled Guides and in a loud whisper would proceed to give them a rapid list of incoherent instructions such as, 'Start from the second row at the back on the right side of the middle and take in the first and last three rows of the left-hand side aisle.' The Scouts received similarly confusing instructions and the result was a most haphazard offering.

My friend Anna had had the misfortune to be requisitioned by Miss Birch and, before we had finished the second verse of the offertory hymn, a worried expression appeared on her face as she suddenly realized that the row she had just passed the bag down had already received one a few moments before. Grabbing the wooden handle of the bag from a startled parishioner she began to panic while Miss Birch gesticulated wildly with her hymn-book to the row which should be tried next. The sidesmen were upset that their perfectly choreographed collection routine could be reduced to such chaos. At the same time, one ran the risk of incurring the wrath of various officious gentlemen in the congregation who considered it a sacrilege to pass the collection bags with such a lack of decorum. Old ladies, worried that they had been missed out, caught Anna by the arm and whispered in an agitated manner. By this time the bag had mysteriously disappeared into the depths of the congregation. Poor Anna was by now totally confused by all the conflicting advice she had received from Miss Birch, the sidesmen, officious gentlemen and flustered old ladies. The only option left to her was to make a dash for the front row and hope that she caught up with the bag before it was time to hand it to the altar server.

It was the custom on church parade Sundays for various flags to be carried up the aisle at the start of the service. A patriotic Scout headed the procession carrying the Union Jack. He was followed by another

Scout carrying the Scout flag. These flags were tall and heavy and could only be carried in a holster worn by the flag bearer. On occasions it was the responsibility of those in the colour party to give not only moral but also physical support to the flag bearer. Occasionally I carried the Guide flag and I found it was impossible to see what was happening in front of me; it was more by luck than judgement that I never had a collision. Behind us followed the Cubs with an equally large flag and the poor Brownies brought up the rear, ignominiously carrying a plastic toadstool. (In later years this was changed to a brown plastic pennant which looked even more silly.) At the end of the nave the colour parties stopped, leaving a brave flag bearer to make the precarious ascent of the chancel steps alone. The heavy flags, complete with silken tassels, threatened to topple over before they reached their destination, which was the altar rail. The vicar reverently received the flags and handed them to an altar server, who secured them in special racks until the end of the service.

On one occasion a Guide accidentally lost control of her flag and was powerless to prevent it giving the vicar a nasty blow on the head. From then on we were terrified of dropping our flags and the vicar kept his distance. It was also quite a sight to see the vicar reverently clutching the plastic toadstool. The toadstool was made in two parts and had to be handled with care lest the stalk departed from the top. The rather nice plastic brown owl, which usually took pride of place on top of the toadstool, sadly had to be left at the back, sitting safely under the font.

The church would be packed to overflowing on this particular Sunday in the month and while we sat cramped together in the pews I observed my surroundings. The elegant pedestal flower arrangement by the pulpit added an outdoor freshness to the musty, dim interior. Stained glass windows glowed ruby red from the morning sun and threw rainbows of coloured light on to the wooden floor. Shafts of sunlight filtered through the leaded window panes and particles of dust could be seen lightly eddying on an invisible current.

The service continued its well-defined path. We sat, we stood, we knelt. We sang, we chanted, we fidgeted. We felt faint in the musty atmosphere, dropped our collection money and counted the organ pipes. We silently laughed at old ladies' hats, thought about the roast beef for dinner, switched off in the sermon and lost our places in the prayer books. It was with heartfelt relief and a silent prayer of true thanksgiving that we heard the organ start to grind away at the National Anthem and the monotony ended. During the singing of all three verses of the Anthem, the colour parties assembled on each side of the aisle in readiness to collect their flags. Solemnly we traversed the nave with flags nodding and silken tassels taking a crafty swipe at our hats and our noses. As the congregation bowed their heads in final prayer, the vicar took the opportunity to transport himself from his position at the altar to the church door where he mysteriously reappeared. He stood in a pool of sunshine on the church steps and shook everyone by the hand as they left the church. People absently murmured 'Nice sermon, Vicar' and old ladies patted his arm encouragingly. The rest of us, clinging on to our hats, raced out to the main road where the band had reassembled.

We saw the Sunday school turn out, with Miss

Peebles looking somewhat less harassed than usual. This was not surprising since after the Scouts, Cubs, Guides and Brownies had been eliminated from their usual positions in the Sunday school she was left with only a handful of children. The second processional march was short compared with the first one, simply up one road and down the next.

Miss Birch forced her fingers into her leather gloves and reassured herself that her hat was still secured. She gave a jaunty nod to the scoutmaster which said 'Be prepared, I'm about to march' – and she did!

The Summer Fête

The day of the summer fête dawned dull and overcast, the forecast for the day was mixed. The weather proved a bone of contention between those respons- ible for setting up the stalls in the church garden during the morning. 'It's gonna rain before long', was the gloomy prediction of one old-timer. 'Nonsense,' chipped in a born optimist, 'the forecast on the wireless said, "Sun this afternoon with temperatures rising".' 'That'll mean thunderstorms then,' the old- timer replied. 'Unlikely,' shouted an old boy who was setting out the whist-drive tables for use in the tea tent, 'me barometer's rising.' 'Well I reckon as it's broken then,' mumbled Old Tom, 'cos, mine's falling.' The Mothers Union then arrived *en masse* and the men departed to another part of the garden.

It had been suggested that I and a friend should be flower girls in the afternoon and sell buttonholes. This meant we had to help make them up in the morning. Miss Dunn duly arrived in the church hall. Miss Dunn was a stout lady with a most intimidating manner. She was a paragon of the Wives' Group, although how as a spinster she ever gained entry remained a mystery. She was domineering and dictatorial and excelled in upsetting people. On this particular day she carried with her an assortment of roses, asparagus fern, tin foil and a large box of safety-pins. She was just giving her orders as to how we should proceed in making them when Miss Willis, who smelt of lavender and mothballs, arrived carrying a bunch of wilting weigela. She had also brought tin foil and safety-pins. Miss Dunn was not impressed. 'Weigela doesn't last long without water,' she said, staring pointedly at the sad-looking flowers. Before Miss Willis could make her defence Mr Bulmer arrived with a magnificent bunch of pink and white carnations from his allotment. 'Carnations is what you need for buttonholes' he said. Miss Dunn's eyes lit up like cash registers. 'Wait for it,' I thought; I didn't have to wait long! 'We'll charge fourpence for the rose buttonholes and sixpence for the carnations,' she said excitedly (Miss Willis gave a polite cough to remind Miss Dunn of her presence), 'and – er – tuppence for the weigela ones,' she added hastily. By the end of the morning my friend and I were heartily sick of buttonholes. By the time we had trimmed off the thorns from the roses our fingers were bleeding. We then had trouble with caterpillars on the asparagus fern, and despite wrapping the tin foil hard round the base of the weigela stems it was impossible to make them stand up straight. Miss Dunn arranged the buttonholes in cardboard trays which we were to hang round our necks. The carnations were given prominence due to the fact that they were more profit-making and she laid the roses on top of the weigela. After spraying them well with water, she bore them off to the ladies' toilet where it was cool.

Outside in the garden, the church 'Know It All' was fixing up the public address system. It crackled and hissed – then, 'One, two, testing, testing' *crackle, hiss, thump*, 'Testing test . . .', he was suddenly cut off in mid-stream. 'What the –' he began but catching sight of the curate he didn't finish his sentence. It turned out that Old Tom had unplugged him as he wanted to mow a patch of grass and the lead was in the way. Order was restored and off it went again. *Crackle, crackle*, 'testing, testing, testing . . .'

The sun came out in the afternoon as we awaited the arrival of the local dignitary who had the honour of opening the fête. She arrived wearing a vivid green hat with a shocking-pink feather in it. She didn't waste time with a speech but promptly said, 'I declare this fête open,', then had some difficulty cutting through the red ribbon with a pair of blunt scissors. The vicar obviously thought a speech was necessary, so he prepared to deliver one himself. *Crackle, crackle*, went the public address system. 'I do hope', he began, 'that you will all enjoy yourselves and that you will visit all the stalls. We also invite you to the . . .' What we were invited to no one ever found out as at that moment the Scout band started up a loud fanfare. The people moved off chattering to look round the stalls and with a shrug the vicar wandered disconsolately off in the direction of the tea tent.

The stalls were many and various. Each church organization had been assigned one. The Cub master was in charge of the 'Roll a penny' board while a patrol of Scouts presided over the 'Lost Treasure Hunt'. Once, someone forgot to mark the square which contained the treasure so consequently no one won the prize that year. No doubt Miss Dunn would have been delighted at this ingenuity. The Brownies had been assigned the bran tub. Parishioners who had been caught by the bran tub at the church bazaar walked quickly past it, leaving only the uninitiated to explore its hidden treasures!

The men spent considerable time trying to throw rubber rings over various bottles positioned many feet away. As these contained sherry, gin and Southern Comfort it was not difficult to understand their enthusiasm. Knitted dolls, bath salts, baskets of fruit and a teddy bear beckoned from the tombola. There was also the toffee-apple stall. It was perhaps unfortunate that Miss Peebles had been left in charge of this. She shared the stall with Miss Venables who was responsible for the coconut ice. Pink and white slabs were threepence, green minty ones were fourpence ha'penny. A large pile of greaseproof paper was on hand for wrapping up the sweets. Everything started off well, but as the afternoon wore on things got progressively worse.

In the meantime I was busy selling buttonholes to people who didn't really want them. Basically there were three types of purchaser. Firstly the friends of my mother and ladies who had known my grand-mother; they felt it their duty to buy one from me. Helping to pin a buttonhole on to one large-chested, eau-de-cologned old lady, the pin dug into her and she jumped backwards with shock, stepping on the toe of the vicar who was standing behind her. From then on I let people pin on their own buttonholes. The second category comprised patronizing, middle-aged men. 'Hello dear,' they would begin. 'What pretty buttonholes, we must have one of those, mustn't we?' and they would make a great show of pinning them on to their lapels and giving me a wink. The vicar was given one free, because he was the vicar. The purchasers I liked most were the old boys of the parish. They would march up or amble over, such as their infirmities allowed, and whistle through their dentures, 'One carnation please Miss'. I didn't want to charge them. I would have happily given them the buttonholes for nothing, but it would probably have hurt their pride and, besides, Miss Dunn was hovering. Proudly they would pin their carnations on to their lapels, recapturing the dignity of yesteryear, and with their straw hats and clipped moustaches they looked every inch the English Gentlemen that they were as they strolled away.

By now the sun was shining so brilliantly that the temperature was indeed rising. Raincoats were taken off and soon cardigans followed. I think the vicar would have liked to have taken off his cream blazer but it wasn't done. He was slowly turning puce under the restriction of his dog collar. I thought it just as well that he was wearing his straw hat or he might have needed Miss Venables' smelling salts. Back at the toffee-apple stall, the rise in temperature was causing problems. Miss Peebles was having to unstick the toffee apples which had become glued to each other. I pitied the treasurer who would have to count her profits as the threepenny bits were probably also stuck together. The coconut didn't look too good. I think Miss Venables must have dropped some of it because she was now selling coconut-ice crumbs wrapped in a screw of greaseproof for tuppence ha'penny.

Sometime during the afternoon the loudspeaker announced that the judging of the fancy dress contest was about to commence. This took place behind the tea tent. Half a dozen canvas chairs had been arranged in a row and upon these reclined the judges. They comprised the local dignitary, who was still resplendent in her violent hat, sitting between the scoutmaster and Mrs Brampton-Jones. (Mrs Brampton-Jones had been selected merely on the strength of being a cousin, three times removed, of the son of a bishop.) Seated next to Mrs Brampton-Jones was Mr Dodge, a local shopkeeper and on his left was Miss Armitage, the daughter of a retired missionary. Seated at the end of the row was the vicar. He was enjoyably sipping a cup of tea and munching a custard-cream biscuit – he was only there to make up the numbers. Mr Newington raised his hand for silence and asked the children to parade in front of the judges. From an opening in the tea tent there appeared a Red Indian closely followed by a white rabbit, several fairies and an assortment of soldiers. Little Miss Muffet frightened Little Red Riding Hood with her toy spider and Red Riding Hood's big brother, who was dressed as a wolf, was subsequently reprimanded for threatening behaviour as he attempted to destroy the spider. Queen Victoria and Mrs Tiggy-Winkle got the giggles and Lord Nelson burst into tears and ran off to look for his mummy. Sooty and Sweep were the winners. After the prizes were handed out there followed a display of country dancing. I abandoned my flower selling and got ready to 'strip the willow'.

Later in the afternoon I happened to glance over my shoulder and, looking back towards the church, I could see some ominous black clouds building up. Before long, huge drops of rain splattered on to the ground. There was a distant growl of thunder. With a shriek, Miss Venables abandoned her coconut ice and made a dive for the relative safety of the tea tent. At the first drop of rain it was also everyone else's intention to make for the tea tent. Inside, the tea urn was hard pressed to keep up with the demand. As it happened the rain didn't amount to much, although the thunder rumbled around for some time, which meant that Miss Venables refused to leave the tea tent. My mother took a cup of tea out to poor Miss Peebles who was heroically coping with the toffee apples and the coconut ice. 'I don't suppose you'd like to help?' she wearily asked my mother. Looking at the sticky mess, my mother was glad that she could truthfully reply that she was otherwise engaged in the tea tent. With the fall of the rain and the rise in temperature the humidity had also increased and as a result the toffee apples suffered still further. Miss Peebles was now desperately trying to tear off greaseproof paper which had accidentally adhered to them. *She* then became stuck to the greaseproof paper. Many apples now had a most unusual topping of toffee covered in pink, white and green coconut ice. 'You'll have to put those prices down', shouted Miss Dunn, 'or they won't shift.' Next time I went past Miss Peebles, toffee apples were down to tuppence and someone had supplied another tray of coconut ice.

My tray of buttonholes was nearly empty. Early on in the afternoon the old boys had bought all the carnations and my other purchasers had had to make do with roses or wilting weigela. The customers who had bought the rose buttonholes found that the flowers were now drooping and many made it an excuse to hurry off home so that they could revive them in a vase of water. Those with the weigela ones didn't have to bother, as theirs were dead already. Most of the visiting public had now gone home and the clearing up was left to those of the parish who excelled in such matters. Miss Dunn dictated the best way to pack up the tea cups, while she was out-shouted by the church 'Know It All' who was using the public address system . . . *Crackle, crackle*, 'I should like to make an announcement. Will someone pick up the discarded raffle tickets and will someone make sure that . . .' *Crackle* – silence. This time it was no accident; Old Tom had unplugged him on purpose. Miss Venables had to move out of the tea tent because they were pulling it down. Miss Peebles picked up her hat and dusted off some green coconut. Her sticky hands stuck to her equally sticky handbag.

She wearily surveyed the shambles on her stall. The coconut ice had all sold, and all but one of the toffee apples, which was still edible if one discounted the numerous bits of greaseproof which adhered to it. Not wishing to leave it, Miss Peebles picked it up and made a present of it to Miss Venables.

The Guide Camp

I surveyed the conglomorate of objects scattered around my bedroom. There were enough items to equip a full-size expedition to the Himalayas. I was going on an overnight Guide camp. Bring a change of socks, Miss Birch had instructed. I was taking three pairs, just in case. There were a pair of waterproof over-trousers and an anorak. I was ticking the items off my list. One thin jumper, one thick jumper, one very thick jumper, two cardigans. I fell over my wellingtons. There was a most ingenious set of camping utensils which my father had bought for me at the Army Surplus Store. It comprised several billycans and some cutlery which all fitted into a neat lightweight package. My torch rolled off the bed (the bulb never seemed so bright after that but it still worked). I continued ticking items off my list: one woolly hat, one pair of gloves, one woolly scarf. One sleeping bag, courtesy of Stephen's mother; it had arrived with a quantity of mud on the bottom and a note of apology. My mother had washed it and it was now being aired in front of the fire – my mother always insisted that everything was well aired. One sheet sleeping bag which my mother had made out of an old sheet, one map and a bar of soap.

My first aid kit was expanding rapidly; I had recently finished a first aid course and I was aware of all the eventualities which might occur. 'No', said my mother, she didn't have a triangular bandage; use a large headscarf instead. 'No', she didn't have a half-inch, inch, two-inch or three-inch bandage; I would have to make do with a strip of old boiled sheet and a safety-pin. She donated the remains of a pre-war crêpe bandage and a piece of pink lint. I had a tube of antiseptic, tweezers and a sterilized needle. Item after item went in and I wrapped the whole in an old plastic mac of my grandfather's, stuck a large red cross on the outside and attempted to ram it into my rucksack. Unfortunately they were now the same size.

Like all good Girl Guides I was prepared, and carried, as well as the comprehensive first aid kit, four pennies for the telephone should a situation be beyond the scope of the first aid kit, a compass in case we should get lost and not be able to find a telephone box and a whistle to blow should we be attacked by a strange man whilst searching for said telephone box. The whistle could also be used for guiding a search-party should we lose the compass. A clean hanky completed these essentials. Anna always lost her hanky and eventually solved the problem by pinning it inside her knickers. My mountain of essential equipment was far heavier than anything I would be able to carry and sadly I had to revise it.

The day arrived. Staggering under my revised load I collapsed into the waiting coach. Some forty-five minutes later the coach stopped at the end of a wide gravel path and we disembarked. We followed Miss Birch through some deciduous woodland and on to a wide grassy path. At the bottom of the hill we passed a group of Scouts who had set up camp and were now sitting in canoes on the grass. 'Roll!' shouted the scoutmaster and the canoes fell on their sides while the occupants wildly flapped the air with their paddles. Half-way up the steep hill we came to a broad, grassy plateau and the area designated for the Guide camp. Our rucksacks were so heavy we were almost on our knees by the time we reached this point. Miss Birch as well as being called Captain was also known to us as Badger, and her helpers were Mouse and Weasel. Badger Birch now proceeded to bark instructions at us. At some point before our arrival several large canvas tents had been left on the hillside; they were rolled up in canvas bags. 'Each patrol take a tent,' commanded Miss Birch. Throwing our rucksacks in a heap we gingerly approached the bomb-like canvas packages. Later, I was to become a patrol leader, but at that time I was a minion in the Scarlet Pimpernels. We hauled our tent to a suitable-looking patch of ground.

A short while later saw the grassy hillside littered with a quantity of tent poles, pegs, ropes, mallets and canvas constructions in varying degrees of collapse. Badger bashed in the tent pegs single-handed – the ground was rock-hard and none of us had the strength to do it. Every few minutes she shouted 'Mind the guy ropes' as a Forget-me-not tripped over. Eventually the tents were pitched and we moved our belongings under the musty canvas. It was then time for lunch. This appeared in the shape of a huge stainless-steel drum full of oxtail soup which was ladled into our plastic beakers. Strange, thin caterpillars dripped off the bushes and the trees. There was a plague of them. They got inside our hair and into the soup. One girl was sure that Badger Birch actually swallowed one.

In the afternoon we collected firewood. Each patrol had to build a fire on which to cook the evening meal. We formed a few dry twigs into the regulation 'A' shape and attempted to light them. A few wispy smoke signals spiralled into the air and then petered out. We tried again, and again, and again. We were left with a pile of ashes and a few charred sticks. The other patrols didn't fare any better. Badger Birch stomped over, threw a handful of twigs haphazardly into a heap and produced a cigarette lighter from her pocket. She was *prepared*. The flames leapt to attention and soon a good fire was crackling and spitting sparks. The menu was beans and sausages. I didn't risk the sausages; they were black on the outside and raw inside. I made do with a piece of bread and a plate of smoky baked beans, followed by an apple. While the girls were attempting this culinary camping cuisine, Miss Birch unfolded a canvas camping stool and from her rucksack produced a wide-necked flask filled with stew and thus proceeded to fortify herself. Yes, she was indeed *prepared*.

A large camp fire had been built at the lower end of the camp site. It would have been to everyone's advantage if we could have used it to cook the evening meal on; but no, it was designated for singing round only. Badger Birch dragged huge logs round the perimeter for us to sit on. Weasel produced a guitar and we were off on a tour of camp fire songs. We sang about fleas, fleas, with kilts and hairy knees, in the quarter-master's store. We sailed on a boat to China with a cargo of tea. We followed this with a song about fish and chips and vinegar, the second verse of which Badger Birch had banned on the grounds that it was unsuitable gutter-language. A few daring Guides ignored this and soon we were all singing 'Don't put yer muck in our dustbin, our dustbin's full.' Miss Birch turned pink with annoyance. We would make up for our fall from grace with a beautiful rendition of the Swiss Chalet song. We all had fun with the 'You'll never get to Heaven' camp fire song, which contained such verses as, 'You'll never get to Heaven in a biscuit tin, 'cos a biscuit tin's got biscuits in.' Once again we incurred Badger Birch's displeasure by singing another verse which went 'Oh, you'll never get to Heaven in a Playtex bra, 'cos a Playtex bra won't stretch that far.' Miss Birch was possessed of a well-upholstered bosom and the subject was therefore taboo. We drank cocoa and sang a few more songs. The fire burnt low and we shivered. Badger Birch declared it was time for bed.

I climbed into the sleeping bag and was soon intimately aware of every stone, lump, hump, and bump under the groundsheet. I had kept my walking socks on and I now reached out for my woolly hat; it was very cold. The hunched shapes of the other girls shifted about and were then still. The last torch was switched off and the night began. So did the snoring. It was terrible. I was amazed that the female of the species could make such an infernal racket. It surpassed a family of pigs I once knew who used to put themselves to bed at sunset and snored their way through the night. I am a light and silent sleeper myself, or so I've been told, and I knew it was going to be extremely difficult to fall asleep amid such gruntings – besides which, the cocoa had gone through and I wished to visit the 'facilities'.

This was going to be very difficult to put into practice. First of all I had to extricate myself from the sheet sleeping bag which seemed to have attached itself to me as I crawled out of the quilted bag. I tried to be quiet and not create a disturbance. I located my torch which had rolled under the sleeping bag – it was responsible for one of the hard lumps I had been lying on. I crept slowly like a cat towards the entrance of the tent. I debated whether to switch on the torch but decided to attempt my break-out in the dark. How do you silently undo a heavy-duty zip? The answer is you can't. I tried to do it slowly at first but the loud *creak, creak* sounded horribly deafening in the silent night. I then unzipped it quickly and it sounded like a gunshot in the silence. I froze, but all around me the grunting and snorting continued unabated. My fingers fiddled with the knots which tied the tent flaps together. Soon I had made a hole large enough to crawl through and I stumbled out on to the wet grass. Thick clouds scudded across the moon and light was scarce.

At the bottom of the hill there was a concrete building which housed the toilets and washing facilities. Nearer to the Guide camp, by the side of the path, there was also a lean-to shed which housed a most insalubrious, primitive privy. I was quite used to the absolute darkness you can experience in the country and it didn't bother me, but I was not too happy about walking down the long, lonely pathway on my own in the middle of the night in order to get to the toilets. The path was banked on both sides by thin woodland. I did not mind familiar woods at night, but these were strange, dark and creepy. I decided to risk the plague and visit the privy situated on the edge of the camp. Shining my torch on the ground, I picked my way carefully across the minefield of tent pegs and guy ropes. I was wearing an anorak, a nightdress and wellingtons. The hem of my nightdress which I tried to hold aloft soon came into contact with the long, dewy grass. The wind had increased in strength and it began to howl through the tree branches. I reached the privy. It was undoubtedly the filthiest facility I had ever encountered. I will pass over the details; suffice to say I escaped from this primordial privy as quickly as possible. The door screeched on its hinges as the wind blew and I ran as if all the bats in hell were after me. Stumbling back across the grass, I once again froze with fear. An apparition had materialized. It was large, white and wore wellingtons – Badger Birch in night attire. She hissed across the camp, 'Everything all right?' I mumbled a reply, embarrassed at being discovered, and hastened towards my tent as Miss Birch continued to hiss, 'Mind the guy ropes.' I did notice, as I passed within a few feet of her tent, that *she* had a camp bed made up with sheets and eiderdown.

I disengaged myself from the anorak and welling-tons and climbed back into my sleeping bag. The hem of my nightdress and my socks were soggy with dew. I wondered how likely it was that I would get pneumonia. Mr Newington, our hypochondriacal churchwarden, would have known. The torch stuck into my neck and I put on my gloves; it was still very cold and . . . I wanted to go *again*! I decided that one expedition a night was quite enough and I attempted to burrow down inside the sleeping bag to get warm. As I lay there I heard a splat, splat sound on the roof of the tent. This was followed by ping, ping and then ping pong, ping pong. The wind had brought the rainclouds. Soon a loud drumming began as the rain bounced off the canvas. Most of the snorers awoke. We remembered Miss Birch's instructions that we were not to touch the canvas if it rained as the water would come in if we did. We moved our belongings away from the sides of the tent. Several girls hit their heads on the canvas and it was not long before damp patches began to appear. A cry went up from outside. 'Loosen the guy ropes!' barked Badger Birch. It was inevitable that a particularly thick Scarlet Pimpernel would untie the guy rope completely so the front of the tent sagged inwards. I huddled up the far end in my sleeping bag wondering if daylight would ever come again. Miss Birch dealt with the erring Pimpernel and restored the tent to its proper proportions. The snorers resumed their grunting. A long, long time passed and then I heard the 'coo-coo' of a wood pigeon. Day had dawned.

Wearily I crawled out of my sleeping bag and peered out of the tent. Badger Birch was munching a sausage sandwich. She had been down to the Scout camp to collect the milk, and the scoutmaster had presented her with it. *We* only had cornflakes. Later in the morning a watery sunlight filtered through the clouds and Badger Birch set off uphill with us in tow. Her thick tweed skirt swung crazily from side to side, while the rucksack on her back bounced heavily up and down in time to the rhythm of her footsteps. She was soon way ahead. The incline was very steep and we scrambled up, using our hands. At the top we collapsed beneath the gorse bushes. Miss Birch was enthusiastically pointing out certain landmarks and was soon making off for a distant 'trig' point. The Scarlet Pimpernels busied themselves looking for rabbit holes, the Snowdrops had a hat-throwing contest and the Forget-me-nots got lost. This was just before the mist came down.

The view silently disappeared and the world became muffled, white and cold. Miss Birch loomed up through the murk wielding an outsize compass. She rounded everyone up, including the Forget-me-nots who had been discovered wading through a dew pond, and we set off to follow our leader. We circled the gorse bushes and Miss Birch consulted her compass again. We circled the gorse bushes once more and then began to descend a narrow, steep pathway which had been made by sheep and rabbits. We went down and down until the path widened into a steep, quaggy bridle-way, where I sank into a thick muddy ditch. My foot left my boot standing in the mud and before I realized what had happened I put my bootless foot on the ground and my sock squelched deep into the mire. It took great acrobatic skills to liberate my lost wellington as I had to stand on one foot, stretch forwards and haul the errant boot out of the mud. Sussex has been notorious throughout the centuries for its muddy highways and byways and I now had a greater part of it adhering to my person.

We eventually made it back to camp in time to pull down the tents and pack our rucksacks. We stamped out the glowing embers of the campfire and made sure we left no litter. We descended the hill and passed the Scout camp. They now had some real water in which to practise their canoeing. The deluge of rain in the night had run down the hillside and straight into the Scout camp at the bottom! This time the scoutmaster was shouting 'Bail!' as the Scouts emptied the water from their tents with billycans.

We boarded the waiting coach, liberally depositing mud all over the inside. Miss Birch made a quick count of her 'gels' and then we were off home and looking forward to a warm bath and a soft bed.

The Curate

Excitement in the church was rife. Old ladies twittered and whispered to each other that the new curate had arrived. I don't remember any curate before the ruddy faced Mr Albert Crumpton – they had come and gone in total obscurity. Mr Crumpton was a confirmed bachelor who had now taken up residence in a dingy house in the High Street which was reserved for unfortunate curates. He was always dressed in a voluminous black cassock, topped by a highly starched dog collar. My mother, who had had it on good authority, told me that he lived almost exclusively on cheese sandwiches. We also understood that he was looked after by a spinsterly housekeeper whose sole responsibilities were the cheese sandwiches and the dog collar.

The first Sunday he made his official appearance we viewed him with interest and speculation. It was, as everyone pointed out, unfortunate that he appeared to have High-Church tendencies – he had been seen to genuflect on more than one occasion. It was hoped that these and other High-Church habits would be dropped once he'd been influenced by us and the vicar. Not so, he set about trying to change *us* and what better place to start than confirmation classes.

It was given out on a Sunday morning that confirmation classes would begin on Thursday evening at seven-thirty sharp and that they would be taken by Mr Crumpton. The vicar was obviously delighted to discharge this particular responsibility on to his curate and the curate was equally delighted at the prospect of a chance to influence young minds.

And so it was that on a dark, stormy, November night I found myself outside the church at seven-thirty sharp – but the church door was locked. A few other hopefuls arrived and we waited. A ferocious gale tore along the path, whipping through the privet. It howled and whistled round the corners and we buttoned our coats tightly and put up our hoods. We could hear the wind singing in the telegraph wires along the main road. The moon, obscured by storm clouds, gave no light and we waited in near-darkness. Our only illumination was a weak beam of light from the street lamps in the road, which penetrated along the church path only as a ghostly glimmer. We were surrounded by menacing shapes and grim shadows which were stealthily silent in the noisy night. A tremendous roaring surged through the high branches of the oak trees above our heads; shrieking and screaming the gale sought to tear them limb from limb. The storm raged until it reached a shattering crescendo. This, then, was the scene into which there silently appeared, as if from nowhere, a black, hooded figure. The wind attacked his voluminous black garment which billowed alarmingly. The figure had swept out of the inhospitable night like a bat from the underworld. Nervously we exchanged glances with each other. It *was* Mr Crumpton, wasn't it? A jangling of keys added to the Transylvanian scene and we wondered if it might be a good idea to go home. But no, it was indeed Mr Crumpton. After a few unsuccessful attempts to unlock the church door, first with the vestry key and then with the key to the poor box, he finally, by luck, found one which opened it. Thankfully we moved into a sanctuary of peace.

Following a damp, wind-blown Mr Crumpton down the aisle to the vestry, we glanced nervously about us at the ghostly shadows beyond the wall arches. Once ensconced in the vestry, Mr Crumpton resumed normal proportions again and we all breathed a sigh of relief.

I don't remember learning much about confirmation itself, but I do remember the unimportant details. There was the cracked green plastic beaker filled with water which stood on Mr Crumpton's desk. From time to time during his discourse he would pause and take a draught from the beaker. He explained that he had to drink when the weather was 'umid. It seemed impossible for Mr Crumpton to say humid with an 'H' and it fascinated me. I spent each class in eager anticipation, waiting for him to say the word. He usually obliged.

We had a guided tour of the church and admired the Bishop's Chair. Mr Crumpton then seated himself in it with dignity, ostensibly to show us what the bishop did at confirmation, but I suspect he had secret desires of promotion. He instructed us on the intricacies of receiving Holy Communion and what to do if you had a cold or other infectious disease.

Mr Crumpton was a big hit with the old ladies of the parish. He visited them in the week and drank endless cups of tea. He listened to descriptions of their ailments and they fed him dainty sandwiches. They complained about draughts in the pews and he listened patiently while he nibbled sponge fingers. The vicar was only seen on Sundays and special occasions, but Mr Crumpton was often spotted sedately walking the streets of the parish visiting his old ladies. Occasionally he was seen whizzing along at speed on an ancient bicycle. He would be grimly hanging on to the handlebars while his cassock billowed out like a parachute behind him. Arriving at his destination he would swiftly jump off the saddle and he and his bicycle would loose momentum together and crash-land safely at an old lady's gate. Miss Venables had many a cosy tête-à-tête with him, while Miss Peebles kept him amply supplied with buttered crumpets, which made a pleasant change from the cheese sandwiches.

My mother and I wrote a song about Mr Crumpton which we sang lustily to the tune of the 'Vicar of Bray', the words of which are lost in antiquity.

Mr Crumpton was with us for many a year. Finally, though, his High-Church leanings got the better of him and, with a word in the bishop's ear, he was promoted to the status of Curate in Charge at the church of St Lupus in the Marsh, somewhere out in the country, where he was allowed to genuflect in relative obscurity until retirement.

The Youth Club

At one point during his long stay in our parish, Mr Crumpton was given leave by the bishop to go and look after a very frail and elderly sick relative, and this was followed by a three-month sabbatical. In all, he was away for nine months during which time the bishop sent a replacement curate. We had to wait a few weeks before the new one arrived and during that time the vicar found it incumbent upon himself to carry out all the duties of a curate as well as his own. The vicar was a tall, ungainly individual in an ill-fitting clerical suit. He was ethereal and vague and the parish of which he was in charge presented to him an eternal mystery which he never solved. The curate's duties included visiting the sick and the vicar found himself involved in yet another facet of parish life. He normally only had contact with his parishioners from a distance and had not built up a curate's immunity to their ailments. This was how, after only two sick visits, the vicar went down with German measles and a heavy cold. Consequently, he was out of commission for the next three weeks, so the bishop sent a succession of geriatric clergy who had been dragged out of retirement to take the Sunday services, and the old and sick were left to pray for themselves.

The new curate arrived just as the vicar was losing his spots. The Reverend Hector Hardwick made his début riding into the parish on a large motorbike. He wore a leather jacket and a white crash helmet. The vicar was unable to communicate with the Reverend Hardwick, as laryngitis had set in after the heavy cold. It was left to Mr Bulmer to initiate the new curate in the perplexities of the parish. It soon became evident that something entirely new had descended upon us. The Reverend Hector Hardwick was one of a new breed of curates. Miss Willis made this discovery when she was sorting altar linen and the curate appeared wearing an Aran sweater and a heavy wooden cross which hung from a leather cord around his neck. Miss Dunn announced to the Wives' Group that 'He's got one of them guitar things.' Miss Dunn heartily disapproved of what she considered pop-music instruments in church. All explanations regarding David playing stringed instruments in the Old Testament fell on deaf ears and she refused to change her mind.

One Sunday the new curate joined forces with Miss Venables in the Sunday school and they performed a Negro spiritual together. Miss Peebles sat tight-lipped throughout, then she proposed we sing 'Forty days and forty nights' which put a real dampener on the occasion. After two verses Miss Venables jazzed it up on the piano and the Reverend Hardwick twanged his strings in a calypso rhythm and the hymn was sung as it had never been sung before, or since. At the end Miss Peebles slapped her hymn-book down on the altar and asked the Spotty Youth to read a passage from Ecclesiastes and, in like vein, the morning continued. I'm not sure who won in the end.

The parish became quite divided as to how we should address the new curate. Up until that time the curate had always been respectfully referred to as Mister and it went against the grain to call him by his Christian name which is what the Reverend Hardwick had requested. Miss Willis in her customary manner of disgust referred to him throughout his stay with us as 'The Reverend' and in so doing she imbued him with the complete anonymity she felt he deserved. Miss Venables on the other hand took great delight in referring to him as 'dear Hectie', which made Miss Peebles feel sick. A few, like Miss Dunn, called him Reverend Hardwick but the majority, for whom old habits died hard, called him plain Mr Hardwick. Mr Newington preferred to take the middle road and referred to him as the Reverend Hector.

Hector had friends at a Christian commune which had set itself up in a large country house a few miles away. From time to time these friends drifted into the service smelling of goat dung and wearing home thonged sandals. Miss Dunn tried to get them evicted, but the vicar preferred to let them come, seeing it as a charitable act on behalf of the parish. However, I think the Jonah Christian Commune thought they were doing *us* a favour by attending our services. The Reverend Hector Hardwick was extremely handsome and was possessed of a very deep voice which made Miss Venables go weak at the knees. His charm radiated throughout the parish and it was not long before he had almost every female eating out of his clerical hand, the exceptions being, of course, Miss Willis and Miss Dunn.

The vicar put the new curate in charge of the recently formed youth club, where he was known to the female contingent as Heavenly Hector. Our youth club had a personality crisis. It was old-fashioned at heart but felt it had to make an attempt at being trendy. It failed painfully. After evensong a handful of us would congregate in the church hall. We would stand around trying to appear inconspicuous. The church hall was large and echoing with so few people in it. The electric lighting was yellow and very dim. One day a scratched table appeared in the middle of the hall with a table-tennis net fixed across it.

The green netting was full of holes; it had been found in a dusty cupboard – an old remnant of a past jumble sale. It was rumoured that the Mothers' Union might patch up the holes with a bit of crochet but this did not materialize. A couple of boys would irresolutely pick up the table-tennis bats and attempt to hit ping-pong balls at each other. The hall was always icy cold on a Sunday evening as, after the morning's Sunday school, the radiators were turned to low and only emitted enough warmth to stop the pipes from freezing. We would huddle together and shiver. The coffee should have warmed us up but as it was virtually undrinkable only those with strong constitutions and defective taste-buds participated. It was served up in chipped, thick, white tea-cups – Miss Dunn had relegated the worst of the crockery to the youth club. It was the colour of liquid mud and was so strong that the caffeine content was probably over the legal limit. Large globules of undissolved dried milk floated sluggishly over the surface.

Someone had supplied a record player and from time to time one of the latest hits would echo round the building. No one danced. We were all extremely cold and bored stiff and after a while gave up all pretence of enjoying ourselves. We only went because it was the thing to do and we felt obliged to support it. There was also a slight chance that one week something exciting might happen. An improvement did occur with the arrival of Heavenly Hector. He would perch on the edge of the stage and serenade the ladies with his guitar, and lead evangelical choruses written by his Jonah Commune friends.

In the winter we all stayed well in the middle of the hall, fearing that if we strayed into the gloomy recesses we would fall prey to the spectres which we felt were waiting there to get us. A cold, evil, north-east wind would shriek outside and the door locks would rattle unmercifully. The dim electric lights would flicker and it would feel as if the phantoms were drawing ever closer. On one such winter's evening we were treated to some excitement that we could have done without.

Heavenly Hector, attired in a fawn lambswool sweater, faded jeans, sandals and dog collar, was attempting to be one of the lads by joining in a game of table tennis. It was not the sort of game where anyone kept count of the score but the Reverend Hardwick was undoubtedly losing abysmally as the ping-pong balls bounced merrily past his bat and off the table every time. We girls were debating which one of us was brave enough to venture into the dark kitchen to put the kettle on to boil. We had just decided that there was safety in numbers and that we would all go, when we heard a roaring sound from outside. It was definitely not the wind. There was a sudden crash as the doors burst open and a gang of sullen youths stormed in. The ringleader pushed himself forward, chewing gum in a menacing manner. With his hands in his pockets he swaggered across to the table. The table-tennis players melted away towards the walls, leaving the Reverend Hector Harwick to face the enemy alone.

Moving the gum to one side of his mouth the ringleader spoke, 'This is a youth club ain't it; well we've come along to join.' His henchmen moved up behind him. There was a moment of quiet, while as one man they noisily sucked on their chewing-gum and eight sets of molars chomped like a herd of cows chewing the cud. This ceremonial rite completed, the ringleader said, 'See you've got girls 'ere then.' The eyes of his gang turned in perfect synchronization towards us. We backed away into the dark kitchen which until a few moments ago had been a place of phantoms, but now afforded us a haven of security as we merged into the darkness. The gang spread themselves out around the table, trapping the Reverend Hardwick in their midst. All the time the youths eyed everyone and everything up and down, making an assessment as to where the best and most entertaining damage could be caused. The curate introduced himself and the ringleader, still gazing around, said, 'Blimey wot a shower!' Hector very politely continued, 'This youth club is for members of the church only and I shall have to ask you to leave.' One youth dropped a ping-pong ball on to the floor and, as if in reply, he ground it flat with the heel of his boot. Heavenly Hector nervously fingered his dog collar. 'Wanna get rid of us do yer?' said the ringleader, as he walked round the curate. ''Ear that boys? This parson don't fancy our company. Wot we goin-a-do about it?' As one man they withdrew their hands from their pockets to reveal clenched fists. Heavenly Hector decided it was the right moment to preach the gospel. He had taken one of the Jonah Commune tracts from his pocket and was about to present it to the youth when, suddenly, the lights went out. The vicar had for the third time in as many Sundays plugged in an antiquated, faulty electric fire in the vestry and fused all the lights. The swaggering and chewing stopped instantaneously. The gale shrieked like a banshee outside and the hall doors banged. There was a second of silence during which the ringleader shouted 'It's haunted!' and there followed a mass stampeding of boots.

A couple of choirboys, well versed in the fused lights routine, opened a cupboard under the stage and took out a powerful torch which was kept there amongst the trestle tables. The beam of light revealed Heavenly Hector on his knees giving thanks for deliverance and the last of the youths disappearing out of the door. It had taken just thirty seconds of darkness for the youths to be stripped of their swaggering arrogance and to metamorphose into frightened lemmings. We heard motorbike engines roar off into the distance.

Hector went upstairs to rescue the vicar who would be wandering around the draughty church with a candle wondering why the lights had gone out. On subsequent Sundays, the curate locked the hall doors and we all felt much safer. Mr Bulmer replaced the lead on the vicar's lethal electric fire and to the vicar's amazement he was spared further post-evensong perambulations around his church in a mystifying darkness. By the time the summer came, the episode had melted into past history and the doors once again remained unlocked.

It was rumoured that Heavenly Hector was engaged to a girl in the parish – he had been spotted having very intimate conversations with her behind the rhododendron bushes, but this still did not stop him fraternizing with the young girls of the youth club. One night he chatted up my friend Anna, and she fluttered her eyelashes in return. That evening *I* was walked home by a short, fat eleven-year-old who had gained admission under false pretences. As I recall, he had a passionate interest in catapults and other evil devices and was, he told me, intending to become a curate. I managed to lose him by taking a short cut through a twitten, and he wandered on alone, still listening to the sound of his own voice.

The curate continued his romance behind the rhododendrons until St Swithun's Day, when he eloped in a rainstorm on his motorbike with an agnostic. He instantly broke the heart of every spinster of this parish and we had a very wet summer. Anna declared herself devastated and announced that she would enter a nunnery. This idea lasted the best part of a week, until a noble Scout rescued her Guide hat from a puddle and asked her to help him erect his ridge tent. With the departure of the handsome Hector, there was only one eligible bachelor left and he was none other than the Spotty Youth from the Sunday school. I can even now see him coming down the road towards me, his acne wondrously illuminated by the setting sun.

Christmas

Each Christmas my mother faced the problem of 'The Pot Plant'. Each year the problem presented itself in the form of *Solanum capsicastrum* or, to put it another way, in the form of my Great-auntie Flo. Every year Great-aunt Flo took it upon herself to present a plant to the church.

Great-aunt Flo was a large lady given to wearing astrakhan hats pierced with large pearl-headed hat pins, and enormous glittering brooches which she pinned to her overcoat. She suffered a heart condition and high blood-pressure but despite warnings by the doctor and the family she refused to stop rushing about. Thus it was that at eight-forty-five on a Monday morning (when my mother was in the middle of the weekly wash) Great-aunt Flo would navigate the steep hills and arrive in a state of near collapse on our doorstep. Without fail she would be accompanied by two large baskets. The visit would put my mother at least an hour-and-a-half behind schedule and she would find she was still feeding wet washing through the wringer when she should have been putting the baked potatoes in the oven. Consequently we would end up with mashed potatoes for dinner instead.

Auntie was a very generous person. She seemed under the impression that we starved in our house (completely erroneously I must add) and it was this false impression which led her to pack her baskets full of food and hump them up the hill.

On arrival she would puff and pant her way into our front room and deposit herself on an upright chair. She would decline to remove her overcoat, saying she wasn't stopping long. Opening her baskets she would proceed to dump the contents on the table: two tins processed peas, two tins Bartlett pears, two quarter-pound packets of tea, a packet of iced biscuits and some oranges. There would also be a pile of women's magazines. At Christmas time the food supply was supplemented by a pound of Brazil nuts (every year we mislaid the nutcrackers), a box of sticky dates and some revolting figs.

Great-aunt Flo was good at talking and while my mother was looking at all the food and saying 'You shouldn't have . . .' Auntie had opened her commodious handbag, pulled out her knitting, and to the clatter of knitting needles she proceeded to tell my mother the latest family gossip. While Auntie clicked away at her knitting, the minutes ticked away on the clock. Auntie's fingers were knobbly with arthritis but it didn't seem to affect the knitting. Neither did her new false teeth affect her talking. A while back she had had every tooth in her head removed by the dentist at one sitting and had been fitted with a gleaming set of upper and lower dentures of which she was extremely proud – and these clicked along in time with the needles.

Three weeks before Christmas she would arrive with an extra bag, and peeping out of the top would be *Solanum capsicastrum*. "Ere's the plant for the winder,' she'd say to my Mother, dumping it on the table along with the processed peas. *Solanum*, for the uninitiated, has red berries. Auntie always selected one which still had green berries on so that it would ripen and be at its best at Christmas. In actual fact the ripening process always took longer than Auntie had anticipated and by Christmas the berries were usually only a pale, yellowy orange. They didn't become bright red until sometime at the end of January, that is if the cold hadn't killed it off by then.

When Great-aunt Flo had finally departed for home, the berry plant would be deposited in our hall in the hope that the warmth and sun from the window would assist its ripening. For the next few weeks leading up to Christmas we just hoped that Auntie wouldn't drop in and see the plant. She expected it to go straight to the church. It went when my mother had time to take it.

If my mother happened to visit Auntie Flo sometime at the end of November, events were slightly different. Under desperate protestations from my mother, Auntie would insist on filling up my mother's basket with the usual items of food and would then press half-a-crown into her hand and say, 'That's for the plant; you can get 'em at Greenwoods.' Greenwoods was the local nursery and my mother had to buy the plant when she next went shopping. If my mother was ever tempted to purchase a prettier plant she never gave in to it. Neither of us took to *Solanum* very much, probably because he was a plant of contention. Auntie never went into the church but there was just the chance that one day she might change her mind and if the plant had not been in the window we would have been in trouble.

And so it was that on a cold, dull, December afternoon we transported *Solanum* to his new home in the church. At this time of year the church was cold and gloomy. Our footsteps echoed on the wooden floor. We just hoped we would find a suitable container for the pot plant in the flower-vase cupboard. My mother yanked the handle; the door refused to move. It frequently got stuck but sometimes Miss Dunn locked it. In those days the church itself was unlocked in the daytime and no one thought of vandals, but the gold plate had recently been stolen from a neighbouring church and Miss Dunn was taking no chances. Personally, I can't see how any self-respecting burglar would have profited from verdigris-covered flower vases, rusty chicken wire and mould-covered saucers. There was a particular green pottery bowl that always suited our requirements, and after turning out half the contents of the cupboard we would usually locate it hidden at the back behind the enamel water jugs. During the weeks leading up to Christmas and afterwards my mother had the unrewarding task of visiting the church frequently to see to the needs of *Solanum*. Considering the cold in the church he managed to consume vast quantities of water. Some years he didn't quite make it to the red berry stage as the cold killed him off. If we were lucky this happened after Christmas and not before. Unlike the mammoth efforts of Easter and Harvest, the church windows were decorated spasmodically during the weeks leading up to Christmas.

Into the silent gloom of the church, parishioners would appear, muffled against the cold and clutching armfuls of holly or yew. They would proceed to arrange these with haste before their hands turned blue and their feet became as cold as the stone pillars which held up the church. During a cold winter the birds ate the holly berries long before Christmas, much to Miss Dunn's annoyance. Consequently, most window arrangements consisted entirely of shades of green, augmented only by the cracked willow-pattern dishes they were arranged in.

Miss Peebles created an arrangement of yew and fir branches and added a few pine-cones for effect. Miss Venables was quite peeved about it. She would have liked to have sprayed the cones with silver paint and added a few glittering baubles, but both old ladies knew that Miss Dunn would not have approved. A few of the more wealthy parishioners dug into their pockets and purchased the odd Christmas rose and yellow or white chrysanthemum. These were given pride of place at the foot of the pulpit.

Each year the crib made its appearance. It was always set on a table to the left of the font. Year after year it mysteriously appeared, and some time in January just as mysteriously disappeared. It was quite large and inside were a collection of pottery figures. They were well worn, with colours which were faded or in places had flaked off altogether. The manger held the pottery figure of a baby which was totally out of proportion to the manger into which they had squeezed it. The unrealistic figures were arranged haphazardly around the stable. Wise men in faded red and purple leant precariously against shepherds who sported chipped pottery beards. A shepherd boy dressed only in a short-sleeved tunic was totally incongruous with the thick layer of cotton-wool snow which covered the stable roof. There was only one thing which gave it any authenticity and that was the straw. Real straw covered the stable floor. The straw lent atmosphere. You could touch it (although adults said 'don't') and it conveyed far more reality than the jaded pottery figures. It was somehow a bridge spanning two thousand years. The chipped ox and the faded, grey donkey who stood up to their knees in straw seemed to say, 'this is what it was *really* like'. I must admit the straw in the church crib had probably been around as long as the figures; it had long since turned from golden to a flattened, dull grey, but nevertheless it did convey reality.

Miss Dunn did not like the straw. She said it made a mess on the floor. However, it gave her something new to complain about for a few weeks and made a pleasant change from her usual comments on undusted church pews and grease marks on the altar cloth caused by dripping candle wax.

Occasionally, whilst attending *Solanum*, we would catch sight of the organist shivering his way to the organ loft. Once there, he would blow a year's covering of dust off the carol books and, after a few preliminary warming up noises reminiscent of a roaring rhinoceros, the organ would thunder into action. The organist pulled out several stops at random and a fanfare of disconnected notes ricocheted off the walls while the ground vibrated. The playing sounded as if the organist was still wearing his woolly gloves – and who could blame him!

Miss Peebles conducted her own musical rehearsals. Each year this consisted of teaching a number of her Sunday school pupils to sing 'Little Donkey'. Someone dressed as Mary would be told to lean on someone else who was on all fours being a donkey. Joseph, meanwhile, tripped over his staff. Invariably the Three Kings would find their crowns were too large and kept slipping over their eyes. The crowns were gold and glittery, and stuck all over with coloured beads – Miss Venables had made them. Disgruntled shepherds could be heard asking in loud voices whose silly idea it had been to make them carry fluffy toy lambs. It had been Miss Peebles' idea but she was too busy to hear as she was trying to restore order amongst a giggling throng of angels. The Spotty Youth was dressed as the Angel Gabriel. He was trying hard to bring some measure of seriousness to the rehearsal by giving a Shakespearian rendition of the verse 'Fear not . . .' which sent the angels into more paralytic laughter.

Miss Peebles was nearly in tears. 'Children, we must get it right and you're not going home until it is right.' For the umpteenth time everyone would chirrup the words of 'Little Donkey' while Mary and the donkey, who was fast wearing out the knees of his trousers, would grudgingly shuffle once more across the hall. All would be well until one of the partially sighted kings collided with a shepherd's crook and fisticuffs would ensue with fluffy lambs flying in all directions. Into all this the words 'I bring you glad tidings', would ring out from the now frustrated acting Angel Gabriel. This would prove too much for Miss Peebles.

Miss Venables sat at the piano, safe and secure on the stage. Misty-eyed she tinkled 'Little Donkey' murmuring it to herself; often she would break into 'Gloria in Excelsis', oblivious to the shemozzle going on in the hall below. 'Piano!' Miss Peebles would shout, and Miss Venables, looking startled, would gather herself together and join the rest of us as we went into the ninetieth rehearsal of Miss Peebles' version of a nativity play.

Somehow everything sorted itself out by the Christmas Eve service. The windows took on the appearance of an indoor forest, the organist discarded his woolly gloves, Miss Peebles had had her hair permed and Miss Venables had dug out her musty fox-fur and draped it round her shoulders. To the accompaniment of a choirboy's croaky solo rendition of 'Once in Royal David's City' the parish was launched into Christmas.

The Daffodil Expedition

March had indeed come in like a lion. The wind was still blowing ferociously as Easter approached. It did not, however, deter the daffodil expedition. Each year on Good Friday we went to pick wild daffodils with which to decorate the church for Easter. An old Colonel, who lived about fifteen miles from the church, owned a large country estate and each year he allowed us access to his woods to gather the masses of wild daffodils which carpeted the woodland floor. The Colonel was an old friend of the vicar. The Colonel's land was all private property and contained no public footpaths, so we were not depriving anyone else of the pleasure of these flowers, and I hasten to add we never dug up the bulbs.

After a hurried lunch, parishioners made their way to the church carrying wicker baskets, scissors, balls of wool and secateurs (these were used for cutting catkins). A coach was due to arrive at two o'clock to take us out to the Colonel's estate. Miss Birch, haversack on her back, huddled into her anorak and joined the others who were sheltering out of the wind round the side of the church hall. Miss Dunn carried enough baskets for several people while Miss Venables had amassed many balls of wool with which to tie up the bunches of flowers. Miss Peebles arrived in a pair of wellingtons and a bright blue, plastic mac from Woolworth's. She was closely followed by Mr Newington who was busily swallowing travel sickness pills. Old Tom arrived. I think he only came for the outing because he said, 'If you thinks I'm goin' to pick any of them flowers, you're wrong, 'cos I ain't,' and he blew on his mittened fingers to encourage the flow of blood through his old veins. By now it was five minutes past two; there was no sign of the coach. The vicar arrived wearing a brilliant green and yellow muffler round his dog collar. The vicar didn't pick flowers either but came each year to visit his friend the Colonel.

Miss Birch consulted her watch; it was now ten minutes past two. She conferred with Miss Peebles who also made it ten minutes past two. 'Oh, jolly good,' said Miss Birch, 'thought me watch had gone wrong.' Mr Bulmer didn't think it good at all because there was still no sign of the coach. He strode up and down peering into the distance, but all he got for his pains was a strong wind in his face and his eyes watered.

Mr Turner and Mr Mitchell had an argument about coach companies. Mr Turner strongly maintained that they would have done better to have had Cuthbertson's Luxury Coaches because they always arrived on time. He said in a loud voice for all to hear, 'I did make this point when I attended your last PCC meeting but none of you on the committee would listen.' The coach company they had insisted on using was Murphy's Express. 'I'm sure the driver will make up for lost time once we're out on the country roads,' countered Mr Mitchell, 'these modern coaches can move pretty fast.' Miss Venables turned pale; she didn't like fast vehicles. At the thought of Murphy's Express driving madly down winding country lanes, Mr Newington took a second dose of his travel sickness pills.

The curate had come to see us off. Mr Crumpton did not personally indulge in daffodil picking. He would spend the afternoon visiting a few bedridden old ladies and drinking cups of tea in front of glowing coal fires. Just then we heard a blaring horn and Murphy's Express screeched to a halt. It turned out that the driver had had to stop at a garage because the radiator had been leaking, but it had been patched up and Mr O'Reilly, the driver, was sure it would last till we got back. Miss Venables became all flustered; 'I really don't think we ought to travel in that,' she twittered to Miss Peebles. Before Miss Peebles could answer, Miss Dunn butted in 'Come on, get on board everyone, we've wasted enough time already.' It did not do to argue with Miss Dunn, so everyone obediently filed on to the coach. The vicar sat in front with Mr O'Reilly and chatted to him all the way. There was a slight hiatus when Miss Venables discovered that her seat was over a rear wheel. 'I can't travel over the wheel,' she said with panic in her voice. 'Why?' asked Mr Turner, 'frightened it's going to fall off?' This put new ideas into Miss Venables' head and she started reaching for her smelling-salts. Miss Peebles stood up for her friend, 'She can't travel over a wheel because it makes her feel queer.' 'No more queer than she is already,' muttered Mr Mitchell. Another seat was found for Miss Venables nearer the front. Being in closer proximity to the vicar, she felt much safer.

Everyone waved out of the window to Mr Crumpton and the coach moved off. I understand that strong winds can affect people's temperaments and I think that this was to blame for the bad mood everybody was in. Roger and Stephen from the Sunday school had been allowed on the outing providing they behaved themselves. Miss Birch had already cuffed them round the ears twice because they wouldn't sit still in their seats.

After the coach had been going for some time, Mr Bulmer began to get apprehensive. The driver really was taking a most unusual route to Old Mill Woods. Mr Bulmer went forward and tapped Mr O'Reilly on the shoulder. 'Excuse me,' he said 'but

are you sure you know the way?' 'To be sure' was
the reply and Mr O'Reilly indicated a scrap of paper
which passed as an invoice stuck on the dashboard.
'Destination', it read, 'Cold Hill Woods'. 'But that's in
the opposite direction,' expostulated Mr Bulmer. He
was turning a most alarming colour of puce. 'Old Mill
we wanted!' he shouted, stabbing the invoice with
his forefinger. By now Mr Turner had joined him
at the front. 'What can you expect from Murphy's?'
said Mr Turner. 'You've got it all wrong,' Mr Bulmer
shouted at Mr O'Reilly; 'We want to go to Old Mill
not Cold Hill.' 'To be sure oi've got it roight,' said Mr
O'Reilly; 'I wrote it down meself.' 'Well, there's your
answer,' groaned Mr Turner. 'Turn this coach round
immediately!' shouted Mr Bulmer. At this point the
vicar intervened, trying to pour oil on troubled waters,
and said, 'Mr O'Reilly has been telling me all about
his prize-winning rhubarb, most informative.' 'Blast
his rhubarb,' muttered Mr Bulmer under his breath
in a most un-Christian manner. Mr O'Reilly good-
naturedly executed a three point turn in the narrow
lane, sending the back end of the coach down into a
ditch before revving the engine and shooting off back
the way we'd just come.

Finally we arrived at Old Mill Woods. The Colonel
was leaning on a gate marked 'Private' awaiting
our arrival. Miss Dunn arranged the unloading of
the coach and soon everyone was following the
Colonel into a 'Trespassers will be prosecuted' area.
Mr O'Reilly stayed in the coach with his thermos flask
and a copy of *Sporting Life*.

It was sheltered in the woods; all we could hear
of the gale was its roaring in the high branches.
Sunlight flickered through the trees and it danced
and leapt in a seemingly never-ending variety of

intricate patterns which threw themselves on to the muddy woodland path. We crossed a little bridge and here the path forked. Everyone continued straight on with the exception of the Colonel and the vicar who turned right and headed in the direction of Old Mill Hall for the ever-important cup of tea.

At one point we had to leave the wood and walk along the side of a ploughed field. To gain entry back into the woods we had to cross a stile. Miss Peebles, not used to navigating in a pair of wellington boots, had some difficulty with this, but Miss Dunn pushed from one side while Mr Turner pulled from the other and soon she was over. In this part of the wood ran a stream. It flowed from the Old Mill down through the woods; it was fast flowing and, owing to the winter rains, the water level was high. Soon we came to where the daffodils grew in profusion. They were short-stemmed with small trumpets of a pale, primrose yellow. Now the picking could start in earnest.

Miss Venables wasted no time and was soon bent double over the yellow carpet. Miss Birch gathered a few bunches together in no time at all and was about to shove them into her haversack when Miss Dunn intervened. 'You'll squash them!' she said in a horrified voice. 'Here you are, put them in one of my spare baskets.' Miss Birch did as she was bid, then wandered off with her secateurs for the more important job of cutting down any catkins which grew low enough for her to tackle.

We had left Old Tom sitting on the stile in the sunshine, sucking contentedly at a tobacco-less pipe. Miss Venables was happily talking to herself as she neatly tied up her bunches of flowers with the wool she had brought. 'No, I don't think the red,' she murmured; 'it clashes with the green stems. Maybe the blue or the pink? No, definitely not the pink.' She called across to Miss Peebles, who was gathering daffodils by the bank. 'Do you think grey or brown would look best?' Miss Peebles, who was used to her friend's eccentricities, called out, 'Brown'. This was followed by a strangled cry, a splash and a loud 'Help me someone, help me!' Miss Venables rushed over to the bank where a few minutes before Miss Peebles had been busy picking. Miss Peebles was now in a very ungainly position. She had one leg in the water, the other dug in half-way up the muddy bank, while with her hands she hung on to some tussocks of marsh grass. She was completely stuck, she couldn't pull herself out, and she was certainly not going to let go. Miss Venables wrung her hands in distress and burst into tears. 'Get help!' panted Miss Peebles. Miss Venables rushed towards Miss Dunn waving her arms; then she remembered she was frightened of Miss Dunn and changed course and ran towards Mr Mitchell. 'Miss Peebles is drowning!' she cried. Mr Mitchell closely followed by other parishioners made for the stream. Mr Mitchell pulled off his anorak as he ran along. He was about to remove his sweater and plunge in to the rescue when he saw a bright blue mac clinging to the bank. 'She exaggerated as usual,' gasped Miss Peebles. Willing hands soon pulled Miss Peebles back to safety and sat her down on a fallen log. Miss Peebles removed one of her wellingtons and tipped out a bootful of muddy stream water, some frog spawn and a few pebbles.

This greatly appealed to Roger and Stephen who had watched the proceedings in awed silence. If Miss Peebles could go paddling then so could they. They had an inkling at the back of their minds that the adults might not approve (adults rarely approved of anything) so they walked further down the bank and stopped behind a large willow tree. They had decided to keep their boots on as Miss Peebles had done, and soon they had scrambled down the bank and were happily splashing in the stream. They would probably have got away with it if Stephen hadn't tripped over a boulder and fallen headlong into the water thereby soaking himself from head to foot. Miss Birch, who was wielding her secateurs not far away, heard the splash and went to investigate. Stephen was duly hauled out and severely reprimanded and Roger got a cuff round the ears for collaboration. By now everyone else had arrived to see what all the fuss was about. Miss Venables burst into tears again at the thought that one of her nephews had nearly been drowned. A best friend and a nephew all in one day was really too much. 'Get those wet clothes off him', instructed Miss Dunn, 'and if anyone's got any clothing to spare, give it to me.'

Stephen was dried down with Miss Foggerty's flannel petticoat and Miss Dunn dressed him as best she could. Miss Birch donated a spare pair of socks and Mr Newington, who was wearing several pullovers as a precaution against the March wind, took one off and handed it to Miss Dunn. It was a large pullover and reached to Stephen's knees which was fortunate as no one had any spare trousers. Miss Venables wrapped a silk scarf round his neck and someone produced a woolly hat and a pair of mittens. Mrs Pettigrew had a red plastic mac in her bag and this was put on over the jumper. It threatened to trip Stephen up so Miss Venables hitched it up round his waist with a length of pink wool. Like Miss Peebles, he had to put his wet wellingtons back on his feet.

Miss Birch then played chase with the boys, in and out of the trees, to keep them warm. Mr Newington walked with Miss Peebles back to where they had been picking flowers. Miss Peebles' boot squelched as she walked. Mr Newington regaled her with the story of a cousin of his who had gone paddling in the sea at Ramsgate in February. 'Caught pneumonia, she did,' informed Mr Newington; 'then she went funny after that and had to be put away,' he added darkly. This gave Miss Peebles food for thought, especially as she could feel the damp rising from her wellington.

Miss Dunn was once again busy picking daffodils. With all the interruptions she was becoming anxious lest not enough flowers were picked. Looking around, she felt quite deserted. Miss Birch could be heard thundering through the undergrowth with the boys; Miss Peebles was lost in reverie; Miss Venables was sitting on a log caressing a sprig of pussy willow while she recovered from her double shock. The men had gone off in search of catkins. Miss Foggerty was attempting to dry her petticoat on a tree branch – and Mrs Pettigrew? Well, Mrs Pettigrew was writing poetry. Perhaps I should explain about Mrs Pettigrew.

Mrs Pettigrew was an extremely tall lady who carried herself with great dignity. She was married to a high-ranking Civil Servant. Exactly which department her husband was in we never knew. It was rumoured to be the Foreign Office. He didn't come to church and she rarely referred to him. She carried about her an air of having had a mysterious past but she never allowed anyone to get close enough to find out any details. She favoured Harris tweeds and pearls. Her grey hair was neatly coiled into a bun. She also had what my Mother called one-o'clock feet.

Her feet, clad in Clark's size nine, best black lace-ups were turned out at a permanent angle. Her feet were so large that it was difficult not to stare at them. As I said, Mrs Pettigrew wrote poetry and she was at it now – scribbling in a little notebook which she kept for this purpose. She was busy writing an 'Ode to the Catkin'.

Presently, the sun went in and a chill wind rustled through the woods. Miss Dunn pronounced it was time to go home. Gathering up baskets of daffodils and carrying twigs of catkin and pussy willow, everyone trotted off to the waiting coach. We collected Old Tom on the way. In answer to Miss Dunn's sarcastic remark that she hoped his afternoon had been fruitful he replied that the sun had done wonders for his rheumatics.

We arrived at the gate marked 'Private'. There was the coach, but there was no sign of Mr O'Reilly. Miss Dunn shouted for him. As he didn't appear Miss Dunn shepherded everyone on to the coach, which had been left unlocked. Minutes later Mr O'Reilly appeared, looking rather furtive and clutching a parcel wrapped in newspaper. He disappeared round the back of the coach and reappeared a few seconds later, minus his parcel. He jumped up into the driver's seat and turned on the ignition. Mr Turner suspected he'd been poaching but he had no evidence with which to tackle him. However, on the way home, several people seated at the rear of the coach could smell a distinct fishy odour mixed with exhaust fumes and Mr Turner felt his suspicions were not without foundation.

The coach doors shut and the engine juddered and rumbled. The coach bounced backwards then forwards as Mr O'Reilly experimented with the gears. 'Oft we go!' shouted Mr O'Reilly, but was forestalled by a twittering old lady who seemed to be saying something about a vicar. It was Miss Venables who had noticed that the vicar was not in his seat. Miss Dunn was on the point of mounting an expedition to search for him when we caught sight of a green and yellow muffler hurrying between the trees. A few seconds later the vicar appeared, breathless and apologetic. He was helped up into his seat and Mr O'Reilly, who was anxious to be off before anyone else was discovered missing, let go the handbrake and we shot forward into the road, the wheels sending a shower of mud into the air and caking the already grimy windows. Fortunately, the windscreen stayed clear. Soon we were bouncing and rolling along the lanes towards home, poached eggs and hot cross buns.

Easter

It was Easter Week and the vicar had taken himself off on a five-day retreat. Before he went, he arranged for his charismatic friend, the Reverend Poddlewell, to take the Maundy Thursday service. This was a sombre occasion, when the gold cross on the altar was covered over and we sang mournful hymns. It was very popular.

On this particular Maundy Thursday evening we were met on our arrival at the church by a transformation. Half the pews had disappeared and the nave was blocked by a very long table, upon which stood a profusion of flickering candles. Apart from the porch light and one over the hymn-book table, the rest of the church was in darkness. The voice of Old Tom could be heard saying, 'It's just like going to the pictures.' We stumbled over a few fallen hassocks and made it to one of the remaining pews. 'Sacrilege!' announced a dominant voice and in the candle-light we could see the gloved finger of Miss Dunn pointing to a fat, brown, cottage loaf sitting on the table. I am sure that Miss Peebles was thankful for a Communion without wafers. The rice paper had a habit of sticking to the roof of one's mouth and it usually took the whole of the Communion hymn to unstick it with the tongue, grimacing grotesquely in the process. On the frequent occasions when Miss Peebles lost the wafer behind her plate there would be much clicking of dentures under cover of a lace hanky.

One year, the Spotty Youth decided to follow Mr Crumpton's normal Passiontide practice of fasting. His stomach rumbled throughout the service and he crammed the rice wafer into his mouth like a starving man. If he had fasted the year we had the Reverend Poddlewell to take the service, I think the cottage loaf would have proved too much for him. Alongside the brown bread on the table were two bottles of Communion wine; the normal glass decanter had seemingly disappeared with the pews. The gold chalice had been allowed to remain and it glittered brilliantly in the light of the candles.

The Major was handing out hymn-books and commenting, 'Don't know how you're going to see to read these.' Miss Venables, true to form, had already dropped hers, along with a pair of gloves, and was now grovelling in the dark under the pew. Mr Newington peered at his prayer book in the darkness, a worried expression on his face. He took his reading glasses on and off several times. It was obvious that he feared a deterioration of his eyesight, which of course had nothing to do with the dimness of the church.

The organ grunted and grumbled, then stopped. The choirboys had obviously stuck chewing-gum up the *vox humana* again. Young Miss Armitage flopped down breathlessly beside us and proceeded to peel glue off her fingers. She had undoubtedly been indulging in her hobby of collage making. There were probably black-eyed beans in her bag and split peas in her purse. The organ made a second attempt which was followed by a very distant strangled cry as the organist discovered more pipes affected by chewing-gum.

The stout figure of Miss Dunn, clad in a camel-hair coat, cast sinister shadows on a stone pillar. Mr Bartholomew, an elderly widower, waved his hymn-book romantically in the candle-light. Its effect on Miss Venables was lost as she was still crawling among the hassocks. Miss Peebles returned the gesture with an icy nod, which I don't think Mr Bartholomew received as it was too dark. A waft of heady perfume came to me on an updraught. Mrs Pettigrew always smelt as if she had bathed in incense. The organ squeaked and rumbled into life, then stopped. There followed a fiercely whispered conversation after which the organist hurried between the choir stalls, caught his foot on an unseen object and prostrated himself before the altar. We didn't see him for the rest of the service, he must have left by a side door. It later transpired that the Reverend Poddlewell had alternative Maundy music plans which did not include an organ.

The church held an atmosphere of anticipation, almost of excitement. The table was covered with a large, starched, white sheet and the elegant, golden candlesticks with their high, tapering candles stood majestically upon it. The Reverend Poddlewell descended the chancel steps, a very tall man with a magnificent stage presence. His white vestments rustled as he walked up the nave and the scent of ecclesiastical mustiness ascended my nostrils. The Reverend Sydney Poddlewell stood before the table; his soft brown eyes gazed kindly upon us. He then raised his hands and shouted 'Praise the Lord!' Miss Dunn's mouth worked overtime; she seemed to be trying to speak but no sound came out. From the Lady Chapel came the distant tones of two violins, a guitar and an oboe playing 'Loving Shepherd of Thy Sheep'. Slowly the sound came nearer until the Elisha Quartet appeared at the end of the nave. They were from Mr Poddlewell's church. The music ended and was followed by an atmospheric hush. Suddenly the door from the porch burst open and Miss Birch blew in saying loudly, 'Has there been a power cut?' The heavenly atmosphere was abruptly brought down to earth and Miss Birch was hastily

ushered into a back pew by Mr Bulmer. The Reverend
Poddlewell continued with the service. We sang two
hymns unaccompanied and largely by memory – it
was too dark to read the print in our hymn-books.
The first and last verses were easily remembered but
the ones in the middle were a jumble of disjointed
words and phrases which we strung together in a
semblance of the original as we followed a few words
behind one of the older choirboys who had a loud
voice.

During the service the Elisha Quartet said 'Praise
the Lord!' every so often, which made Miss Peebles
jump, Miss Armitage giggle and Miss Dunn furious.
The Reverend Poddlewell gave a truly marvellous
sermon. He preached in a way we had never been
preached to before. He brought the gospel to life
and the candle-lit tableau of the Last Supper set
before us spoke to us of the reality of our faith.
We took Communion in silence. Miss Venables was
completely overcome and, having been influenced by
the Elisha Quartet, she called out, 'Praise the Lord!'
Miss Peebles' embarrassment was almost palpable.
The final benedictions concluded, the congregation
filed quietly out of the church to the sound of the
Elisha Quartet playing 'When I Survey the Wondrous
Cross'. Most of us hoped it would not be long before
the Reverend Poddlewell visited the church again.
Even Miss Dunn must have been impressed with the
money saved on the lighting bill.

On Good Friday we went as usual to pick daffodils
and on the Saturday we decorated the church. The arrangements consisted of yellow catkins which dropped pollen everywhere, daffodils, quantities of moss
and Miss Venables' favourite, the pussy willow. We
would both stand and stroke the soft, furry, grey buds

whilst flower-arrangers' bedlam raged round about us.

On Sunday morning the vicar was back in his normal place and the Easter Service went like clockwork. We sang all eleven verses of 'Hail Festal Day' and to Miss Peebles' joy we also sang 'Jesus Christ is Risen Today'. We would sing this in the Sunday school for as many weeks after Easter as Miss Peebles could decently get away with. We might as well have sung Handel's Hallelujah Chorus and been done with it. 'Jesus Christ is Risen Today' consists of three verses, each of four lines. After each line one sings an Alleluia which takes up ten notes. This is repeated twelve times – a total of one-hundred-and-twenty syllables. One day Miss Peebles discovered another hymn in the Ancient and Modern, which could be sung at Ascension, entitled 'Hail the Day that Sees Him Rise' and realized that it could be sung to the same tune as 'Jesus Christ is Risen Today'. From Miss Peebles' point of view it was even better – it contained six verses, which meant twenty-four Alleluias, each of ten syllables, comprising a total of two-hundred-and-forty notes! We went home with Alleluias on the brain; they had only just begun to wear off when Sunday arrived and we were ready to be brainwashed all over again. If Miss Venables played the piano she would play the Alleluias quickly and get them over with. If the Spotty Youth was in charge, the hymn would be played in slow time as this was as fast as he could manage, and the half-hearted Alleluias would grind on for a century.

At Easter the congregation was a sea of hats. Miss Dunn would be wearing what appeared to be a basket of fruit. Miss Venables would leave her brown felt hat in the wardrobe and wear instead a creation of netting and swansdown. Miss Peebles favoured feathers and Miss Armitage would wear something bright, soft and woolly. Mrs Pettigrew used to arrive in a large-brimmed, Ascot concoction while Miss Birch, who rarely wore hats, would have rammed a peaked hat of brown corduroy over her straight hair.

There would be so many people in church on Easter Sunday that the Communion would take a long time to distribute. My mother would have visions of the roast beef in the oven shrinking to nothing. Both the vicar and Mr Crumpton administered the chalice to parishioners personally and it was considered indecent to touch it yourself. One of the dangers of sitting in the back row was that you would be last up for the Communion. The chalice would be almost empty and Mr Crumpton in his enthusiasm to drain the last dregs down your throat would tip the cup up so that it collided with your front teeth and crashed into your spectacles. Occasionally the red wine would be so far down the chalice that all you would receive would be a mouthful of air and a resultant hiccup. During a busy service such as Easter, the servers used to help out and, as they had not had Mr Crumpton's High-Church training, they used to hand the cup to you so that you could cause your own damage to your teeth and glasses.

The church would be hot and stuffy with so many bodies congregated together and we would be gasping for fresh air. Once outside, the cold north-easterly wind, which was usually blowing at that time of year, would take away the little breath we had left. The path would be packed with parishioners and by the time we'd said hello and goodbye to everyone on the way, the roast beef would have shrunk still further. Prior to acquiring a moped, Miss Birch often used to walk down past the woods with us. Hilary Birch strode everywhere at a cracking pace which my mother didn't mind because it meant we got a move on. Miss Armitage, on the other hand, used to walk very slowly because all her energy and concentration went into talking.

We would leave the vicar sheltering in the lea of the church porch vaguely shaking hands with his parishioners – he recognized very few of them. Mr Crumpton would remain inside the now empty church, genuflecting to his heart's content.

The Jumble Sale

At the previous meeting of the Parochial Church Council, members had agonized for two hours on how best to raise much needed funds for the church. It had been extremely cold in the church vestry and their brains had become as numb as their hands and feet. The warmth from the single-bar electric fire did nothing to alleviate the cold, mainly because the vicar had stretched his legs out in front of it and his cassock effectively prevented the heat from spreading through the room. The long-established resident of the mousehole in the wainscoting was the only other recipient of the warmth and no doubt he toasted his toes with as much indulgence as the vicar. The idea of a jumble sale had been suggested by Mr Bulmer, but his idea had been dismissed by the others as being unoriginal and too much like hard work. However, after two hours in near-arctic conditions no one had come up with a better suggestion and Mr Newington, who was suffering badly with his chilblains, was by then ready to agree to anything. Thus it was finally decided to hold a jumble sale; the vicar agreed and Miss Whitticks scribbled it down in the minutes for posterity. It was to be in aid of church funds with ten per cent of the proceeds going to the Zambezi Mission run by Miss Tennyson, late 'spinster of this parish'.

The Scouts were dispatched with a handcart and an old pram to gather up any particularly unwieldy items that might be donated. The Scouts decided to start their collection in the wealthier part of the parish and they trundled their handcart up and down gravel drives, collecting items which seemed far too good for jumble. Such articles included Axminster carpets, solid oak wardrobes, reproduction paintings, sheepskin rugs and even a black-and-white television set. This was in the days when such things were considered a luxury. The Scouts managed to cover nearly all the roads in the parish and could be seen most evenings pushing a top-heavy handcart in the direction of the Scout hut. A sample selection of their plunder included, amongst other things, a rusty iron bedstead with broken springs, an armchair with the stuffing falling out, a striped mattress, a chipped garden statue of the wine god Bacchus and a cracked aquarium. Perching precariously on top could be seen a dilapidated rabbit hutch. These were all deposited under lock and key in the Scout hut. Soon, bags, boxes, trunks, sacks and tea-chests full of jumble began to accumulate. Each Sunday the infant Sunday school which met in the hut found less and less room to sit down until on the Sunday prior to the jumble sale they had to be evacuated altogether.

The jumble sale was due to start at two o'clock on the Saturday afternoon. Saturday morning was bedlam. The men dragged out the trestle tables and erected them round the hall, then the jumble flowed in, along with the helpers. Soon the contents of the bags and boxes had been tipped out on to the floor ready for sorting. Miss Peebles was on bric-à-brac and she pounced like a magpie on anything that wasn't clothes or books. The churchwarden, assisted by the Scouts, was responsible for selling large items from the stage. These items included several wireless sets, labelled, 'working', 'not working' or 'in need of attention'.

The curate, who was running the second-hand book stall, was extremely alarmed when he recognized an item on the stage as being one of his own possessions and most definitely *not* one he had donated. Leaning against an over-stuffed horsehair sofa was his bicycle. He had left his bike propped up in the privet outside the hall door as usual, but an over-helpful Scout, not knowing this was the curate's normal practice, thought it had been left by a kind parishioner as jumble. It was an ancient, rusty machine and the mistake was quite understandable. In his hurry to retrieve the bicycle before it was sold at a knock-down price, the curate jumped up on to the stage. In doing so he was neatly tripped up by his cassock, collided violently with a large standard lamp and finally came to rest on one knee in a tin bath. The large, fringed lampshade narrowly missed Mr Bulmer and came in to land on top of the piano. The chattering in the hall below ceased abruptly and there followed a stunned silence. The curate, now extremely red in the face, was helped to his feet by Mr Bulmer, and the bicycle and the curate were assisted off the stage. A few minutes later the curate was spotted tying his trustworthy machine to the church railings with a length of rope. Attached to the handlebars was a notice which read 'Not for Sale'.

Miss Venables arrived with a large bag of jumble; she had obviously been busy turning out. Her jumble was old enough to be antique and caused considerable laughter behind her back. We unpacked a stone hot-water bottle, a button hook, a fur collar which appeared to have mange, a fusty lace bed jacket and a grotesque china ornament in the shape of a snarling dog. Miss Willis also arrived clutching a big bag. All the clothes in it had been neatly washed and ironed and they exuded an overpowering odour of lavender and mothballs as did Miss Willis herself. Even the faded, romantic fiction paperbacks and the cheese grater could be attributed to Miss Willis by their distinct aroma. Miss Willis was given an iron rail on a stand at one end of the hall and upon this she hung many coathangers. When anyone discovered an exceptionally good item of clothing they would hand it to Miss Willis for inspection. If it passed the test it went on to the rail and acquired a price tag of 2/6d or more. She refused outright to sell ladies' trousers.

The curate was fast disappearing behind a mountain of books. Paperbacks with musty, yellowing pages were stacked precariously one upon the other. *Rupert Bear* and *Children's Hour Annuals* he propped up with dexterity against the side of the stack. There were hardback editions of the *Household Encyclopaedia*, spotted with age but teeming with intriguing information of a bygone era. There were numerous books which displayed faded covers with obscure titles written by unknown authors. I purchased an ancient copy of *Enquire Within*. The front cover was missing and the back page which boasted a ready reckoner was hanging by a thread; the pages were covered with brown spots but they yielded a mine of information. I am now fully conversant with how to overhaul a mangle and the correct way to address the eldest son of a duke. The curate stood ankle deep in a swamp of *Reader's Digest*s, historical romances, thrillers, mysteries and murders; he wasn't fussy and continued happily stacking his books.

Miss Birch was trying to match pairs of shoes, ably assisted by some enthusiastic cubs who were treating it like a game of snap. The vicar put in a brief appearance carrying a string bag. This did not contain jumble but the items his wife requested he get from the Co-op. His appearance was but a formality. The Mothers' Union manned the clothes stalls. They allowed Miss Venables to help them as someone had to keep an eye on her. Miss Peebles was too busy tastefully arranging bric-à-brac to take charge of her. She artistically arranged jewellery along the front of the table – it was largely of the glass-bead variety donated by herself.

The two Miss Jameses, retired missionaries of the Zambezi Mission, had felt it their duty to attend to help boost sales and thus assist their dear sister who was at present sweating it out in Africa with the natives. They had been given the toy stall and with the help of the Major they arranged the toys with military precision. Mr Newington's chilblains were by now fully recovered having been subjected to a liberal application of wintergreen ointment. This was just as well because it looked as if he might start dancing at any moment. Someone had donated a radiogram and a pile of seventy-eights and Mr Newington was joyfully trying them out. Miss Venables went all soppy when she heard the strains of 'Hear my Song Violetta' as it wafted through the air across the jumble.

By now the clothes were heaped up on the tables and for the shorter women it was getting difficult to see over the top. The ladies wore overalls and some wore rubber gloves as well. This was a precautionary measure against the plethora of fleas, bugs, moths and nits which they imagined were waiting to pounce from the Everest of clothing in front of them. At twelve-thirty a halt was called for lunch. This con-sisted of vast quantities of soup which was heated up in the tea urn. Once, this had had unfortunate consequences. The soup had been minestrone and had contained bits of spaghetti. The next time the tea urn was used (at the Old Boys' whist drive) they found the spout on the urn was blocked. They attempted to free it with the result that they ended up with spaghetti letters in their teapot. That was the last time *that* particular type of soup was allowed.

At two o'clock battle commenced as the public hurled themselves through the door. Large ladies with enormous bags tore at the piles of clothing. More and more people arrived and threw themselves on top of those already there. They fought and snarled and squabbled, stamped on each others' feet, used language that the curate had never heard before, pulled, shoved, shrieked and shouted. At one point it seemed that the clothing was going to topple and drown the Mothers' Union. Fortunately this catastrophe was averted, but unhappily the legs of one of the trestle tables caved in from the onslaught, with the result that bedspreads, cushions and curtains were now in a pile on the floor. This mishap did not deter the bargain-hunters; indeed, they found it an advantage to be able to wade in on top of the goods. It quite upset poor Miss Foggerty who was behind the table at the time. From then on she was assisted by two strong Scouts.

The toy stall wasn't faring much better. The off-spring of the ladies with the massive bags had made straight for the toy stall. Like their mothers they were seasoned bargain-hunters and attacked the stall with fervour. Soon the thousand-piece jigsaw was scattered far and wide and Meccano scrunched underfoot. Soft toys were eagerly snatched up, and water pistols and table-tennis bats flew across the table. The two Miss Jameses were horror-struck; the tribal uprisings by the Zambezi had been nothing compared to this. Their table was soon a shambles. The Major did his best to protect the good ladies from the flying missiles. From time to time an extremely loud and well enunciated voice would break in above the furore saying, 'This is the BBC Home Service', as Mr Bulmer attempted to demonstrate the working wireless sets. It was somewhat quieter in the book corner. Shy little spinsters with National Health spectacles and woolly hats sorted through the romantic fiction, handing their threepences over to the curate with some embarrassment.

Miss Willis had probably hoped for a quieter type of clientele for her *haute couture*, but it was not to be. Her coathangers were attacked with the same gusto as the items on the more unsavoury stalls. Some people turned quite nasty when they saw the price tags. This was a jumble sale and they didn't reckon to pay above sixpence for anything. They were certainly not going to pay over the odds for the weird assortment of garments which Miss Willis had considered fashionable, however good-as-new they were. Miss Venables had a spot of bother as well. One customer was heard to say 'I'm only givin' you a penny for it; I only wants it for the buttons.' Miss Venables turned pink with indignation; she had originally asked ninepence for the fluffy cardigan. It seemed that the best bargains were always at the bottom and the clothing was turned upside down as people rummaged through. They had only to spot a fragment of bright material to be convinced that 'this was it', the bargain of the year and they would pull at it with force. It was most unfortunate if someone else was tugging at the other end.

Miss Peebles was beaming delightedly behind her junk table, as she collected in money for assorted cups and saucers, cracked plates, useless china ornaments and hideous lampshades. The mothball/lavender cheese grater was sold as was Miss Venables's sepia photograph of a nineteen-twenties charabanc excursion. She also appeared to do a roaring trade in glass beads, sold numerous egg cups, cruets, toast racks, a rusty bird cage and a bath plug. Miss Peebles was not sure if the church hymn-book had got in by mistake. She sold it for tuppence ha'penny.

By three-thirty there was not a lot left. The vociferous Miss Dunn was stationed by the door to deter dealers. There were a few waiting outside restrained only by Miss Dunn's menacing appearance. Before they were allowed in, Miss Dunn let the woollens man in. The woollens man bought any woollen items by the pound and any woolly articles still left on the clothes stalls were bundled into large sacks. This was quite profitable. The dealers were then allowed in. I think they expected to be paid to take it away; there certainly weren't any bargains left. The hall looked as if a bomb had hit it. Clothes, toys, books and items miscellaneous littered the floor. Behind the tables the Mothers' Union wilted. Miss Peebles was busy emptying her Oxo tin on to the floor and counting the takings.

Miss Willis had a slight disagreement with one of the dealers, as she was steadfastly refusing to let go of the remaining high-quality items. She told him in a high, quavering voice that they were worth more than the two shillings he'd offered her for them. The dealer looked a tough character and Miss Dunn stepped in before the argument could go further and said she would take the clothes to the Salvation Army. At the same time Miss Venables piped up that she could take some of them to the orphanage, while the two Miss Jameses volunteered to ship some of them out to the upper reaches of the Zambezi. The angry dealer decided to leave them to it, he kicked one of Miss Foggerty's remaining cushions across the floor, swore at the curate and departed. Soon after that it was time to go home. The helpers looked forward to a nice hot bath of pine essence and disinfectant. They hoped the Zambezi Mission would appreciate their windfall. They couldn't help wondering if it would have been less hassle had they all put some money in the Mission's collecting box instead, but still, it had been fun – hadn't it?

The Harvest Festival

Harvest Festival began as do all good church events, on the Saturday morning. At nine o'clock our house overflowed with produce collected for harvest. Indeed, we could have held our own private Harvest Festival and then distributed the harvest gifts back to the poor and elderly who had donated them in the first place. Let me explain . . .

At around half-past eight in the morning a voice would call, 'Uh-oo anybody there?' and old Dora's face would appear over the fence which separated our gardens. 'Just picked a few things for the church,' she would call to my mother. My mother whose hands were in the washing-up water and whose mind was on what to have for dinner would reply 'Oh, how kind!' She would then leave the kitchen and balance on a couple of strategically placed bricks among the lilies; this enabled her to peer over the fence at Dora. As our houses were built on a hill, Dora's garden was much lower than ours and it was with difficulty that items were passed back and forth. Dora's neurotic dog would throw itself at the fence and handing anything over was usually extremely hazardous. Her garden was a jungle which quite by chance grew all the right things, and at harvest time she surpassed herself. Huge, shiny Bramleys with stalk and leaves still attached would be heaved over the fence, evil-smelling marguerites by the dozen, armloads of golden rod from which we shook the 'blood-sucking' insects and masses of mauve Michaelmas daisies. No sooner had we deposited these in buckets indoors than we would be hailed by the old lady on the other side, already slightly merry from her morning tot of gin. She would holler, 'Dew want summat for the church? You can 'ave some of our pears.' Such imbibing of alcohol was not typical of our neighbourhood, neither was it the type of neighbourhood where you hollered, but someone had to live next door to her and unfortunately it was us. It really was amazing how many people, who normally wouldn't have dreamt of setting foot in a church, fell over themselves to donate items for the Harvest Festival. No doubt it assuaged their guilty consciences. No sooner were the pears picked and put in a bag than a knock at the door would announce the arrival of Mrs Harrison from down the road bearing a large bundle of rhubarb. My mother would then remember that old Mrs Tidmarsh from up the road had offered some flowers and I would be dispatched post-haste to collect yet another large bunch of Michaelmas daisies.

By now bags, baskets and buckets formed an effective barricade in our hall. Vegetables various collected at the bottom of the stairs and these, together with a large bag of harvest gifts forced on us by Great-auntie Flo, completed our ensemble. We would be all ready for the 'off' when my mother would shout, 'The greenery!' and we would rush into the woods behind our garden to pick large bundles of cow parsley. Greenery was of prime importance to my mother's harvest arrangements. Loaded and weighed down on all sides and to cries of 'Did we put the scissors in?' we would set off uphill for the church.

For the purpose of Harvest and Easter, the church was apportioned to various organizations, each army of volunteers maintaining its own strongly defended territory – no ground had been won or lost since time immemorial. The Guides always decorated the church porch, the Sunday school was let loose on the area around the font, the Wives' Group held the rights to the chancel and various church members were responsible for the windows. When the church had been built, individual church members had each paid for a window. From then on they became known as Miss Thomas's window or Miss Martin's window and they or their surviving relatives were obliged to decorate the window recesses at appropriate times of the church calendar. Our window was not, like some, of the stained-glass variety; my grandmother had paid for an ordinary leaded window pane. Each year I faced a dilemma. I was expected as a member of the Guides to help them decorate the porch, as a member of the Sunday school I was expected to assist with the font, but in the end I helped my mother with the window.

My mother and I staggered into the church with our effects. We had passed the Guides in the porch on the way in. Miss Birch was dressed in brown trousers, brown jumper, brown brogues and brown spectacles. Her ample figure perched dangerously on the porch bench as she attempted to festoon greenery over the entrance. Here my mother shed some of her own greenery and off-loaded a few of our Bramleys and we moved into the church. Inside it was a hive of hushed activity; people conducted conversations and gave orders in respectful stage whispers as befits a sacred venue. Hiding behind the large array of greenery I carried, I skilfully managed to avoid Miss Peebles who was trying her best, though rather unsuccessfully, to arrange something festive in the font. Miss Venables, her felt hat bobbing, twittered merrily away in the children's corner doing creative things with chrysanthemums. My mother donated some of our Bramleys to Miss Venables and she happily spent the next twenty minutes arranging them into a pyramid which soon began to resemble the leaning tower of Pisa. My mother was in haste to get to the cupboard which contained the flower vases. Early arrivals had first pick. We were too late for the crystal vases and Wedgwood bowls and had to settle for plain glass vases and cheap pottery. The unfortunates who came after us would have to attempt interesting things with jam jars and chicken wire. Next, we hunted for a jug. Huge white enamel jugs stood at various points around the church, each one spoken for and each one rigorously defended by whoever had fought for it. Mr Bulmer wandered around, looking daggers at anyone who looked as if they might spill water on the nave carpet.

Having been presented with a jug from a kindly neighbouring window arranger, we set off through the vestry and down the spookily winding stone staircase to the hall below. Here we filled it up with water. Returning through the vestry we were likely to catch a glimpse of the vicar, dressed in a black cassock, writing his sermon notes. He hardly acknowledged his flock as they came and went to the watering place. Indeed the church worked efficiently whether he was there or not and, apart from his necessary officiation over the sacraments, he could have been made redundant tomorrow and no one would have noticed. Back at our window once more, we piled the greenery up at the back and arranged the Bramleys equally on both sides complemented by the pears. Specially chosen misshapen vegetables filled the centre. The forked carrots appeared to have arms and legs, the potatoes had ears and noses – and wasn't that large potato slightly reminiscent of Miss Birch? Michaelmas daisies, marguerites, golden rod and dahlias fought for water in the vases, and the rhubarb tastefully arranged in front completed our particular work of art.

Old boys staggered past carrying the best from their allotments. Enormous wax-polished marrows were laid lovingly on the chancel steps, only to be dwarfed by someone's even larger pumpkin. The turnips didn't stand a chance. The wooden floor of the church was, by now, littered with unwanted flower stalks and slippery leaves lying in puddles of water. Miss Dunn would strut round saying, 'All this must be cleared up, it's dangerous,' and a flustered Miss Peebles would go in search of a non-existent broom; Miss Venables, ever eager to please, would scurry around clearing up, usually upsetting at least one person by accidentally bearing a half-finished flower arrangement off to the dustbins under the impression that it was waste. At this juncture the church would begin to empty, each person going their separate way. In the porch Miss Birch had finished attacking boughs of elderberry with her clippers and with a final flourish of golden rod she was finished. She then departed in the direction of the dustbins and could be heard disposing of her rubbish to the resounding crashes of dustbin lids. Thankfully Miss Dunn left as well, having discharged her self-imposed, parochial oversight to her complete satisfaction. She could be seen hurrying down the High Street in an endeavour to catch up with the churchwarden to discuss another little church matter which wasn't quite to her liking.

The window arrangers left, hoping that nothing untoward would happen to their arrangements during the next twenty-four hours. Visions of dying flowers and wilting greenery accompanied them home. One hoped that the rhubarb would stay in its artistic position and not descend during a quiet moment of the service on to an ancient worshipper seated below and, perish the thought, that a Bramley would not career off the window sill and go bouncing down the aisle. Miss Venables too trotted off home, no doubt hoping that her leaning tower wouldn't lean any further and collapse during the night. It would be a shame if this occurred before other parishioners had had time to appreciate its true artistic value. And Miss Peebles? Well I rather think we left Miss Peebles in the broom cupboard.

The Harvest Supper

The day had been warm and full of mellow autumnal sunshine and an equinoctial gale had finally blown itself out. The horse-chestnut trees had released their fruit during the worst of the gale and we eagerly hunted through the carpet of golden leaves for conkers. Most of the prickly, green cases had split open upon contact with the ground and had obligingly spilled their polished chestnut treasure. Beech nuts, bitter to the taste, lay scattered under the beech trees. The squirrels darted back and forth cramming them into their mouths and furiously digging holes in which to bury them. We picked up dry twigs to store in the woodshed for lighting winter fires and we scuffed through the dry leaves picking up conkers, beech nuts and acorns. But now the day had come to an end and there was a frosty chill in the air. A brilliant harvest moon rose majestically in a black velvet, night sky and myriads of stars twinkled in the infinity of the heavens. Here on earth all had been safely gathered in and this could also be applied to the members of the parish who had gathered themselves in the church hall for the annual harvest supper . . .

Trestle tables had been set up end to end, making two long rows down the length of the hall. They had been covered with clean white sheets which acted as tablecloths. The Wives' Group had made small flower arrangements which were placed at intervals along the tables. An odd assortment of cutlery surrounded each place setting. Mine had a chunky knife with G.R.1951 inscribed on it, a bent, stainless steel fork, a hallmarked silver soup spoon and a dessertspoon which bore the inscription 'Jewin Street'. The thick, white, side plates had until recently been the property of Joe Lyons. Miss Dunn had snapped these bargains up at a closing-down sale.

People stood around in groups, wondering if they should sit down at the tables or whether that would seem a little premature. No one liked to be first to make the decision. There was a great deal of clattering and many exclamations coming from the direction of the kitchen. Miss Dunn was supervising. It had been decided at a PCC meeting that the meal would consist of hot soup, followed by a cold meat salad and a dessert. The Wives' Group and the Mothers' Union had joined forces to supply and serve the food. My mother was chosen to wait on the tables because she was small and could easily nip in and out.

Admittance to the harvest supper was by ticket only and Mr Bulmer, who was collecting these by the door, worked out that everyone who was coming had now arrived. The vicar appeared on the stage and after an apologetic cough he asked us to 'please be seated'. There was so much talking going on that few people heard him the first time, so Mr Bulmer banged the piano lid a couple of times and shouted for silence. After making his announcement a second time the vicar said a short prayer of thanksgiving for the harvest and we all asked the Lord that for what we were about to receive He would make us truly thankful. Mr Turner, who had just come out of the kitchen, whispered to Mr Mitchell that from what he'd just seen we'd have done better to have asked the Lord to preserve us. There followed a scraping of chairlegs on wooden floor as everyone pulled their chairs up to the table and sat down. Miss Dunn peered out into the hall then shouted to her staff, 'Serve the soup!' The soup was supposed to be served quickly so that everyone received it piping hot but in the event it took longer than anticipated. It was unfortunate that we had been given the choice between 'harvest vegetable' and 'French onion' soup. People who had ordered the vegetable were served with onion and vice versa so that there was a good deal of soup-bowl-swapping up and down the tables. Some people had changed their minds about what they wanted and soon all the vegetable soup had been served and there remained only the French onion. Miss Venables was served a bowl of this and it caused ructions. Miss Venables whispered to Miss Peebles, 'I can't eat this; onions upset me.' Miss Peebles who was already tucking into her harvest vegetable muttered, 'Dear me', then turned to Mr Mitchell on her left and whispered, 'Do you know anyone who will swap with an onion soup?' Mr Mitchell shook his head but passed the message on to his neighbour, who passed it on down the line. 'I really can't eat this, you know,' continued Miss Venables. 'I shall be up all night and then I won't be able to play the piano in the morning,' she ended as a final threat. By now Miss Peebles' message had arrived at the curate who was sitting at the end of the table. The Reverend Albert Crumpton, distressed that one of his old ladies should be incommoded in such a way, leant across to Mr Bulmer and, after some heated whispering, picked up Mr Bulmer's vegetable soup saying it was more blessed to give than to receive and hurried off to deliver it to Miss Venables. Mr Bulmer muttered something about 'It's a good job not everyone's so fussy about what they eat,' but he didn't look too pleased as he sipped the luke warm onion soup. Miss Venables, now appeased by the vegetable soup and the pat on the arm the curate had given her, ate in silence. Next the cold meat salad was served.

Fortunately these were all the same so there were no squabbles.

For about three weeks before the supper the main topic of conversation had been 'What are you going to wear?' There had been much debate as to whether the hall would be cold and draughty as usual or whether, with all the bodies, it would be hot and suffocating. Most of us compromised by wearing layers that could be removed depending on the temperature. Miss Peebles had made a dress for the occasion. It was of blue tricel, the very latest fabric, and round the neck she had sewn on white cotton daisies. The trouble was that it rode up everytime she sat down and as it did so it revealed her elderly knees. Miss Peebles spent much of the evening tugging ineffectively at the hem trying to cover up her embarrassment. Round her neck she wore a 'diamond' necklace – Woolworth's best. Miss Venables was not so fashionable. She and Miss Willis had both dug deep into their tin trunks and somewhere amongst the mothballs had located their best outfits. Miss Venables' dress was black crêpe-de-Chine and reached almost to her ankles; it had an abundance of black lace and at the neck she had placed a red silk rose. Miss Willis wore a dress of midnight blue taffeta with a profusion of rather limp off-white lace which hung round the neck and cuffs. She wore a double string of pearls round her neck which she patted reassuringly from time to time. Round her shoulders she wore a rather mangy fur stole. Miss Birch had on a thick tweed skirt and a chunky knitted Aran sweater.

After we had consumed our mandarins in orange jelly, cups of coffee were served. There was a slight hiccup when Mr Crumpton spilt coffee on his cassock but Miss Dunn soon had him mopped up and he was sent back to join the fray. Mr Newington generously handed round his indigestion pills and we were all set for the next part of the evening.

Once the tables had been cleared away it was time for the games. Mr Bulmer was in charge. He organized us into six teams and we sat round the hall in our groups. 'Now', instructed Mr Bulmer, 'I will call out an item and the first person to bring it to me will win a point for their team. First I want someone to bring me a left shoe.' Mr Turner was very quick off the mark and ran up to Mr Bulmer holding a left shoe in his hand. He was awarded a point for our team. 'Next item', shouted Mr Bulmer, 'is a nail file.' This was the cue for Miss Venables to empty the contents of her handbag on to the floor. She was still searching for a nail file long after another team had won the point for it, and Mr Bulmer was now asking for a picture of the Queen. Miss Willis rushed up with a threepenny stamp. 'I always carry one with me just in case,' she explained to Miss Foggerty. In case of what I wasn't sure and didn't like to ask, but it had certainly paid off in this instance. 'Next item', shouted Mr Bulmer, 'is the longest piece of hair.' I suddenly found several hands pulling at my long hair. I tore a few out by the roots and the Spotty Youth rushed them up to Mr Bulmer. As my hair was long enough to reach to my waist, we won the point easily. Several more items were called out and there was much general laughter as people rushed up and down to Mr Bulmer. The last item Mr Bulmer asked for was pair of ladies' stockings. This was dreadfully daring. The vicar turned pink and Miss Willis pulled her stole tightly round her shoulders as if to protect herself. Miss Peebles tugged even more ferociously at the hem of her skirt to cover up her stockinged knees, at the same time trying to restrain Miss Venables who was throwing herself whole-heartedly into the game. She was now rifling under her crêpe-de-Chine and umpteen lace petticoats for her suspenders. Miss Willis looked the other way. The Major was the only one to use his brains; he gathered up one of the Miss Jameses and ran up to Mr Bulmer with her in his arms. Amid much applause, he gained the point and Miss James tottered back to join her sister, flushed with success. After waiting sixty-nine years, she had at last been swept off her feet by a man. After all the excitement, Mr Newington handed round his indigestion pills again.

The vicar had made his way up on to the stage. We knew what was coming next from past experience. In the same voice that he used for taking the services he made his announcement. Beaming like an overgrown school boy he said, 'We are now going to play Sausages.' This was the vicar's forte. He arranged us into a circle, all seated on chairs. To those unfamiliar with the game of sausages I shall explain the rules. Each person in turn would be asked a question by the vicar and to all questions one had to answer 'Sausages'. If you laughed or even so much as let a smile begin at the corner of your mouth, you were out. Thus were parishioners eliminated. The vicar began his questioning: approaching Mr Bulmer he asked, 'What did you have to eat this evening?' Remembering the onion soup, Mr Bulmer gloomily replied 'Sausages' and thereby secured his place in the next heat. The vicar now concentrated on Miss Venables; 'What do you wear in bed?' he asked her. 'Sausages!' shrieked Miss Venables, giving way to a spasm of hysterical laughter. The thought of wearing sausages in bed so tickled Miss Venables that she nearly fell off her chair as she rocked back and forth, clutching her stomach and crying with laughter. 'Out!' said the vicar unnecessarily, as it was obvious to everyone that Miss Venables had not passed the test. The vicar then inquired of the Major, 'What form of transport did you use to get here this evening?' No sooner had the Major replied 'Sausages' than Miss Venables burst into more uncontrollable mirth. Her laughter was so infectious that the Major guffawed loudly and was thus disqualified. Mr Turner replied 'Sausages' when asked what he grew on his allotment and Miss Venables had hysterics all over again. Mr Turner, like the Major, became infected and roared with laughter. 'Out!' said the vicar again. It was becoming obvious that unless Miss Venables could control herself she would make the game impossible for everyone. The vicar had now reached Miss Peebles and asked, 'What do you use to brush your teeth with?' 'Sausages,' replied Miss Peebles, staring straight ahead. The thought of her friend using a string of sausages to clean her teeth with set Miss Venables off once more. Miss Peebles, rather embarrassed by the spectacle Miss Venables was making of herself, remained unamused. Eventually Miss Venables decided she needed to get a glass of water and tottered off to the kitchen murmuring, 'Dear me, how funny, how terribly funny.' The vicar continued round the circle, eliminating the odd one here and there. Mr Newington, when asked 'What do you pay the rates with?' replied 'Sausages' then burst into loud laughter as he envisaged himself paying over a pound of pork chipolatas to a surprised clerk at the council offices. The vicar then arrived at Miss Willis. Miss Willis didn't like party games and was finding the whole procedure extremely childish. The vicar had really warmed to his theme now and bounced from foot to foot with unconcealed excitement. The question he put to Miss Willis was 'What do you put in your bath?' 'Sausages', replied Miss Willis icily. And so the game went on; eventually there were only two contestants left, Miss Willis and Old Tom. The vicar said to Miss Willis, 'What might you wear on your head?' Miss Willis gave him a withering look and answered 'Sausages'. The vicar turned his attention to Old Tom and asked 'What do you smoke in your pipe?' There was some hesitation then Tom shouted 'Sausages!' Mr Turner was suspicious; he had noticed that Old Tom, not usually given to anything louder than a mumble, had shouted all the answers. Going up quietly behind him, Mr Turner clapped his hands loudly and shouted 'Boo!' Old Tom didn't bat an eyelid. He had purposely turned off his hearing aid and had heard none of the vicar's questions, replying 'Sausages' as soon as he saw that the vicar had finished speaking. The vicar leant over and adjusted the hearing aid and then disqualified the old rascal. This left Miss Willis. The vicar posed a final question, 'What do you post through a letter box?' 'Sausages', replied Miss Willis frostily. 'I hereby declare Miss Willis the winner,' said the vicar. Miss Willis did not seem enamoured of the honour of Sausage Champion bestowed on her, but was mollified by a tin of Co-op peaches which the vicar awarded as a prize. Later in the evening Miss Willis was heard to remark to Miss Foggerty that the sausage game was really quite an interesting one.

By now it was time for more refreshments. Miss Dunn's slaves came round with plates of cheese straws, sausages on sticks, tea and coffee. After that a queue formed to use the toilet in the choir vestry and we were then ready to face the dancing.

A large wooden box had appeared on the stage and the two churchwardens were busy preparing the record player. The dancing commenced with a waltz. The vicar led Mrs vicar on to the floor and to the strains of 'The Blue Danube' they floated round the hall. Gradually they were joined by other parishioners. Old Mr Bartholomew bowed to Miss Venables and asked her if he might have the pleasure; she fluttered her eyelashes in reply and they disappeared amongst the dancers. I ended up with the curate. I had never been so close to a curate before. He smelt very musty; I think it was the cassock.

The next dance was a foxtrot. Mr Bartholomew and Miss Venables were first on the floor. Mr Bulmer danced with his wife; he kept making peculiar noises, and I overheard his wife tell him it was probably the effects of the onion soup.

Not everyone was familiar with ballroom dancing so a few country dances were included. Soon the music for the Nottingham Swing rang out round the hall. Mr Turner danced with Miss Birch. Her tweed skirt swung merrily from her hips and her outsize, chunky, Aran sweater bounced enthusiastically in time to the music. Mr Turner advanced, retired and 'dosi-doed' making sure that he kept a wide berth of Miss Birch's large gyrating bust. The music ended and the dancers puffed their way over to the chairs for a breather. There then followed another waltz and the now inseparable pair of Mr Bartholomew and Miss Venables floated to and fro, recapturing the atmosphere of times past. Miss Willis, poker straight, held the curate at a distance as they waltzed through the Vienna woods. The sound of swishing taffeta and the aroma of musty cassock wafted over to me as they swept past. During the next country dance, Mr Newington twisted his ankle doing the figure of eight and Miss Dunn shouted at Old Tom because he tried to promenade her when they should have been swinging. It was all too much for the vicar; he took himself off to the kitchen, where Miss James made him a nice cup of tea and let him eat up the remains of the cheese straws.

The next number was a tango. The music was infectious and many couples took to the floor. There, in the middle of them were Mr Turner and Miss Peebles. Miss Peebles had given up trying to control the vagaries of the blue tricel and had now abandoned herself to the music. Surprisingly, she was a very good dancer. Mr Turner tangoed his partner up and down the hall. With arms oustretched they executed the dance steps with military precision. Suddenly catastrophe struck. There was a sound like that of a sudden hail storm and several dancers found themselves hit by hard, flying projectiles. Miss Peebles' string of artificial diamonds had suddenly snapped and the beads rained out in all directions and finally rattled around on the floor. Miss Peebles' euphoria quickly turned to embarrassment. Dropping on to their hands and knees Miss Peebles and Mr Turner tried to gather up the scattered beads, Miss Peebles pulling vainly at her dress once again, attempting to stop it riding up and revealing her underwear as she grovelled around on the floor. Everyone was most helpful and soon nearly all the beads had been found. Miss Willis supplied an envelope and the beads were put in there for safety. Throughout the remainder of the evening people kept coming across beads in the most unlikely places.

After this episode we danced the veleta, which was much more refined. The two Miss Jameses and Miss Willis danced with a genteel aristocratic air. The same could not be said of the gangly Spotty Youth, who danced like a buffalo in rugby boots. The military two-step followed. Mr Bartholomew, Old Tom and the Major were in their element here and saluted smartly to all the ladies. Time was now getting on and Mr Bulmer looked round for the vicar. The vicar usually ended the evening's entertainment with a blessing, but this year no one could find him, so Mr Bulmer just said 'Good-night everyone, we will end with the conga.' The music started and Mr Bulmer set off, closely followed by Miss Venables and Mr Bartholomew. As they passed Miss Peebles, Miss Venables roped her in as well. Next to join were the two Miss Jameses, the Major and Mr Turner. The vicar's wife and Mr Mitchell were added and the line grew very quickly. Further on, Miss Foggerty and Old Tom joined in. The line snaked its way round the hall and came to the kitchen. Round the kitchen we went, picking up Miss Dunn and her merry maids who had just finished the washing-up. Back in the hall we collected Mr Crumpton who tagged on behind Miss Willis who had been caught up in the conga without her consent. Miss Birch grabbed the curate round the waist and hung on heartily as the line hopped into the choir-vestry. Here we found the vicar having another cup of tea, this time with Mr Newington – I think we interrupted an important conversation on nasal decongestants. The vicar put down his teacup and joined in, followed by Mr Newington whose ankle was now much recovered. Mr Bulmer led the way out of the hall door and into the frosty night. We danced round the laurel bushes and circumnavigated the dustbins; we conga'd up the steps and down again; we bounced round the notice-board and hopped through the convolvulus. And on we conga'd under a full harvest moon until Mr Bulmer led us back into the church hall and the harvest supper was over for another year.

The Flower Festival

The Parish had known for some time that the roof was leaking. Those who sat in the back row of the side aisle had known even longer; they were the ones who kept their rainhats on during the service. The organ was in need of attention and the hassocks needed re-covering. All things considered, it was time the church raised some money.

It had been decided by the PCC that the first fund-raising activity would be a flower festival, details of which were pinned up on the notice-board in the porch for parishioners' information. 'Flower Festival', it read, 'We will be holding a flower festival in this church on 1st August. Our theme will be hymn titles. All organizations will be assigned one. We also welcome individual arrangements; parishioners may choose their own hymn titles. All titles must be handed in to Mrs Pettigrew before 20th July, to avoid duplicates and to enable her to write out labels for each arrangement, signed, Ethel Whitticks, Church Secretary.' The PCC was not sure how well this announcement would be received, but need not have worried. The response was absolutely overwhelming. Everyone, or so it seemed, wanted to participate and there was a staggering response in the individual entries. A flower festival committee was set up to cope with all the extra work involved and it seemed no time at all before Friday, 31st July arrived. The church was to be opened for the day prior to the festival so that everyone could arrange their flowers. Many parishioners had taken time off work especially to help, such was their enthusiasm. Friday morning came and everyone made an early start.

Miss Birch approached Mr Bulmer with a request to borrow his wheelbarrow and Mr Bulmer promised to bring it round to the church later in the morning.

Meanwhile, Miss Birch organized the Guides who were supposed to be portraying 'Brightly Gleams our Banner' in flowers. The Guide flag was draped over one of the porch seats; this was a good start but was as far as it went for some time. The idea was to arrange yellow and gold flowers all around the edge to give it a gleaming impression. The problem was how to hide the flower containers. Parishioners passing through the porch on their way into the church offered advice.

Miss Venables came through with a shopping trolley. It appeared to be very heavy and the top was covered over with a large paper bag. Great secrecy surrounded the individual entries. Miss Peebles arrived with a large bunch of ox-eye daisies and pansies but carried as well a mysterious, long package. The Sunday school had their usual area around the font with which to portray the hymn title chosen for them which was 'Behold a Little Child'. When Miss Peebles arrived, pandemonium had broken out. Roger and Stephen had managed to get the lid off the font and were giving everyone a liberal splashing of holy water. Miranda and Alison were fighting over a baby doll that was to be part of the arrangement and, at the moment Miss Peebles arrived, its arm had just been forced out of its socket. 'Children, please be quiet!' hissed Miss Peebles, as she noticed disapproving glances from the other flower arrangers. Miss Peebles handed the daisies to the Spotty Youth with the instruction to find some suitable containers and then tried to organize the children into being *con*structive instead of *de*structive. Her own mysterious package she hid under a pew until she had time to do her individual arrangement.

Back in the porch Miss Dunn had supplied Miss Birch with a large bag of moss which, when spread round the paste jars, covered them nicely. All that remained was to fill them with yellow flowers and the arrangement was complete. 'Company dismissed!' shouted Miss Birch and she rubbed her hands together with joyful anticipation; she had just seen Mr Bulmer arriving with the wheelbarrow.

The Scouts had been given the hymn 'Hark the Glad Sound' and were told to arrange it in a front pew. The assistant scoutmaster, Mr Jeremy Lightfoot, had been given full reign by the scoutmaster who had told him, 'It's more your sort of thing.' Jeremy was a vegetarian bachelor of thirty-five or thereabouts. He lived at home with his mother and they played rummy most evenings. During the daytime he worked as a hairdresser. He was now in his element, delicately spreading a piece of red velvet along the pew. He then began to arrange white roses and love-in-a-mist in a very artistic way. From time to time he stepped back with his head tilted to one side, made a few tutting noises and danced forward again to move a piece of fern a quarter of an inch to the right or left. A few Scouts stood by holding items of essential equipment. One held a pair of hairdressing scissors which Jeremy used for chopping thick stems; another held a pair of embroidery scissors which were used for the fiddly bits – the result was perfection. Jeremy finally gave it a liberal supply of water from his silver mist sprayer and then in front of the completed arrangement he laid a Scout bugle. 'Hark the Glad Sound' was completed. Miss Foggerty looked on enviously; she knew hers would never look anything like that.

The Mothers' Union were attempting to portray 'The Voice that Breathed O'er Eden'. They had arranged many pretty flowers in a garden setting and were now trying to erect an apple branch in the middle of it. The Wives' Group watched pityingly from their place on the chancel steps. Really, the Mothers' Union were not up to this sort of thing. They themselves were portraying 'Guide me, O Thou Great Redeemer'. They had made a signpost out of flowers. It was about four feet high and was indeed a work of art. Meanwhile, the garden of Eden had just been demolished by the apple branch and the voice of Miss Dunn was now breathing over it. 'I think', she commented, 'that it would be best if you cleared all this up and started again with something else.' There was much muttering under the breath at this suggestion but finally they agreed and went away to plan their new arrangement and to ask Mrs Pettigrew to write out the new title for them.

Mrs Pettigrew had been to calligraphy evening classes and she had written all the hymn titles out on pieces of imitation parchment in a beautiful copperplate hand. The parchment was then stuck on cards, which were to be propped up in a convenient position by each arrangement.

Miss Venables was busily unpacking a weird assortment of items from her shopping trolley. Each item was wrapped in a bag. Miss Venables covered her booty with newspaper and then trotted out of the church again.

The Sunday school arrangement had been completed to the best of everyone's ability. It showed a doll dressed in a frilly pink dress, holding a bunch of daisies. The doll stood on the stone surround of the font. Around its feet were arranged bowls of pansies and on either side were tall vases of ox-eye daisies. It was not of great artistic merit but Miss Peebles had something else she wanted to get on with. She arranged the title in front and stood back to survey the effect. At that moment Roger went steaming past, followed by Stephen who managed to stamp in a bowl of pansies on the way, sending a cascade of water all over the hymn title. 'Behold a Little Child' had now become a black smudge. Mr Turner walked past and said 'Suffer the little children'. Miss Peebles gritted her teeth and went off in search of Mrs Pettigrew for another label.

The two Miss Jameses were singing hymns in one corner as they depicted 'Hills of the North Rejoice'. They had erected a quantity of green material as a back cloth and had built up a hill of moss. They had arranged a bowl of flowers to one side of the hill and were attempting to place a compass at the foot of it. They were having great difficulty. They wanted the compass to point north towards the hill but, according to the compass, the hill was in the south. With one accord they moved their green hill to the opposite side of the church and set it all up again.

Old Tom had been saying that he was going to do an arrangement but no one could get out of him what it was. Whenever anyone asked him, he appeared stone-deaf.

The Major had arrived and was pinning up a large Union Jack. Under this he placed a few medals, then he hurried out of the church again. There was a most extraordinary amount of coming and going. The choir had depicted 'Let all the World in Every Corner Sing' and in each corner of the church was a sheet of manuscript paper with the notes of the hymn written on it and tasteful arrangements of larkspur and cornflowers done by Miss Proctor, the assistant organist. Miss Proctor was a small, timid, bespectacled spinster who was usually attired in an anaemic green, gabardine raincoat. She was easily flustered by 'Men of the Cloth' whom she regarded as sacrosanct apogaeic beings with whom she was not entitled to communicate.

The vicar poked his head round the door to see how things were going. The Mothers' Union had now got themselves more organized and had arranged montbretia and marigolds in earthenware bowls and neatly arranged an open bible between two home-made loaves of brown bread. The new title read 'Bread of Heaven on Thee We Feed'.

The 'Hills of the North' were now *in* the north according to the Miss Jameses' compass and Miss Peebles had replaced the smudged label by the font and sent the children home. 'Splendid, splendid,' murmured the vicar, then turned to go out of the church. As he did so, he suddenly found himself under attack. The Major was re-entering the church in a hurry, carrying a sword in one hand and a tin helmet in the other. 'Dear me, violence is not the sort of thing . . .', started the vicar, shaking his head, but he was not able to pursue the matter because he felt someone tugging at his arm. Looking down he saw a flustered Miss Foggerty. Poor Miss Foggerty was not having much success in flower arranging. She had originally wanted to portray 'Hail Festal Day', but had no idea how to go about it. She had attempted instead to arrange a green hill far away. The finished arrangement displayed a tiny piece of moss with a lop-sided matchstick cross overshadowed by a large pink gladiolus. Miss Dunn took one look at it and pronounced it unsuitable and told Miss Foggerty to go away and try something else. Miss Foggerty couldn't think of an alternative so she decided to portray the vicar's favourite hymn. The vicar mused for a while, then said he very much liked 'The Day Thou Gavest Lord is Ended'. Miss Foggerty thanked him profusely and hurried home to gather new material for her second attempt.

The Miss Jameses were now helping the Major out with his display. The sword and tin helmet had been arranged alongside the medals and a large bowl of early yellow chrysanthemums completed the exhibit. The Major produced his parchment label with a flourish; it read 'Onward Christian Soldiers'. He propped it up against the tin helmet and the vicar breathed a sigh of relief.

Miss Dunn was arranging 'From Greenland's Icy Mountains'. She had draped a white linen cloth over some boxes in order to give a resemblance of a snowy mountain, and at the top and bottom she had arranged white and blue flowers which gave it an icy appearance. The whole effect was extremely beautiful. In between attending to her icy mountain, Miss Dunn dispensed cups of tea to the thirsty workers. The vicar, who had the ability to home in on a tea urn from a vast distance, heard the rattle of cups and said, 'Hark the glad sound the teacups come', and with that Miss Dunn arrived and everyone drank a refreshing cup of tea.

Miss Venables had returned with two buckets full of flowers. She then proceeded to unwrap all her paper bags and soon an odd assortment of items began to collect around her on the floor. She unpacked a large stone hedgehog of the variety used for garden ornaments. Next to the hedgehog appeared a camel with 'Present from Egypt' stamped on its hoof. She also unwrapped two china birds, an ancient teddy bear with no squeak, a toy rabbit and a pottery mouse. She arranged them all in a circle facing inwards. In the middle of the circle she created a pedestal flower arrangement and as a finishing touch she gave each animal a buttercup to hold between its paws. The title read 'All Creatures of our God and King'.

Mr Newington arrived with a basket of flowers and a list of instructions (his wife was confined to bed with a virus). The idea had been to portray 'Ride on, Ride on, in Majesty', but Mr Newington was having second thoughts. His wife might have been able to accomplish it but he felt it was somewhat beyond his capabilities. He had gone shopping before coming into the church and some of the flowers were looking extremely sorry for themselves, having wilted in the heat. Mr Newington sat down in a pew and scratched his head thoughtfully. Eventually he seemed to make up his mind and wandered off to Mrs Pettigrew to ask her to write out a new title for him.

Mr Bartholomew was wheezing happily in the Lady Chapel. He had painted a blue background on a piece of board and in front of it he had placed a ship in a bottle. He then wandered off to look for Miss Venables who had promised to arrange the flower part of it.

Mr Newington unpacked his basket. He had some stocks and a bunch of tall blue flowers that he didn't know the name of; they all looked in a very sorry state. Mr Newington begged a few fresh stocks from the Miss Jameses and placed them in a vase of water. He laid the piece of mauve velvet over the box his wife had given him and stood the vase of flowers to one side; in the middle he placed a wooden cross and on the other side he put another vase. This he filled with wilting stocks, collapsed greenery and withered blue flowers. Underneath he placed his new title which read, 'Thou to Whom the Sick and Dying'. He stood back to survey the effect. 'Well,' he thought to himself, 'it's different!'

Mr Bartholomew shuffled over to Miss Venables. 'Lettie my dear, the ship is on the high seas; I wonder if you would come and adorn it for me.' Miss Letitia Venables blushed and allowed Mr Bartholomew to escort her to the depths of the Lady Chapel. Here she proceeded to strew white rose petals over the blue velvet. 'That's the white topped waves,' she explained to an impressed Mr Bartholomew. Next she arranged a bowl of roses and forget-me-nots and together they aligned the title which read 'For Those in Peril on the Sea'.

Miss Foggerty returned. She strung up a midnight-blue curtain as a back cloth. Just as she finished, two Scouts appeared with the forked tree branch thrown out by the Mothers' Union. 'Where do you want it?' they queried. Miss Foggerty asked them to lean it against a pew end so that part of it made a horizontal branch. Then, out of her bag she produced an owl made of felt; she sat it on the branch. After a few moments the owl sagged forward. There was nothing Miss Foggerty could do to make it stand up straight, so the owl had to spend its time on the branch with its beak impaled in its foot – well, it *had* been badly stuffed in the first place. Miss Venables, who was having a lovely time, helped arrange a posy of night-scented stocks and this completed 'The Day Thou Gavest Lord is Ended'. Miss Dunn walked past and commented that it looked more like 'Through the Night of Doubt and Sorrow', but Miss Venables told Miss Foggerty not to worry and that she was sure the vicar would appreciate her portrayal of his favourite hymn.

Mr and Mrs Turner were having a disagreement under the lectern. The title of the arrangement was to be 'Lead Kindly Light, Amid the Encircling Gloom'. Mrs Turner had arranged Japanese Maple, berberis and copper beech in a huge flat dish – this was to be the encircling gloom. So far so good, it was Mr Turner's part that was going wrong. His kindly light kept going out. At the back of the display he had fixed a large torch and the idea was for the light to shine through from the depths of the arrangement. Instead, it flickered on and off for some time and then insensitively extinguished itself. Mrs Turner blamed him for using an old torch. 'I didn't,' snapped Mr Turner. 'It was alright until your mother came to stay and used it.' 'Don't you bring my mother into this,' hissed Mrs Turner. 'You can fix it yourself,' returned Mr Turner; 'I can't stand the hymn anyway.' 'Fierce Raged the Tempest' under the lectern for some considerable time until, by a fluke, the torch light came on and stayed on.

Shortly after that, a distant rumble was heard which grew steadily louder. The rumble was followed by several loud thumps and the church doors burst open to reveal Miss Birch triumphantly pushing a wheelbarrow. In it reclined an enormous boulder. Some of the men helped Miss Birch lift it out. 'I want it just there, by the door,' she puffed. 'It's me "Rock of Ages".' She then proceeded to empty a bag of sand round the boulder and into this she pushed a few flower pots filled with prickly cacti. 'Where are the flowers?' asked Miss Dunn. 'There aren't any, it's the desert,' replied Miss Birch. Only Miss Birch could have got away with it. Actually, it really was quite impressive. There was another arrangement which made an impression on people in a different way.

Standing in an insignificant part of the church was a humble jam jar and in it someone had placed a single dandelion. The caption underneath read 'Just As I Am, Without One Plea'. Its sheer, unadulterated simplicity said far more than a thousand sermons. It moved Miss Venables to tears and Mr Newington had to swallow a big lump in his throat.

Miss Dunn, having completed her icy mountain, now felt it her duty to inspect what everyone else had been doing. Old Tom was dozing in a back pew. Miss Dunn asked him where his arrangement was. 'Up there,' replied Tom, pointing to an empty window. 'But there's nothing there,' said Miss Dunn, annoyed. 'Yes there is,' persisted Tom. 'Alright then, what's it called?' asked Miss Dunn. With a mischievous twinkle in his eye, Tom replied 'Immortal, Invisible', and hurried off down the aisle chuckling to himself. Miss Dunn was not amused. Tom told the joke to several people but no one thought it as funny as he did, as by this time they had all become weary from slaving over their own arrangements. Tom felt that perhaps he ought to do something more constructive. 'Alright,' he said to himself, 'I'll show 'em,' and hurried out of the door to fetch something from home.

Miss Peebles had untied her mysterious package and revealed a long tin tray of the type used in flower troughs. This she proceeded to fill with water. Miss Willis looked a little annoyed; from out of her basket she produced a similar receptacle. Miss Peebles arranged moss and pink and white flowers all around the edge. Miss Willis now looked very annoyed. She too had filled her tray with water, and arranged moss with pink and white flowers along the edge. Both ladies then reached into their bags and simultaneously drew out a bunch of montbretia, complete with long, tapering leaves. Miss Peebles, oblivious to Miss Willis' mounting annoyance, continued to put the montbretia in water. Miss Willis pulled herself up to her full height and marched over to Miss Peebles. 'What's yours called?' she asked abruptly. Miss Peebles rustled around in a large brown bag, took out a carved wooden deer and stood it on the moss. In reply to Miss Willis, she propped up her parchment card among the flowers. It read, 'As Pants the Hart for Cooling Streams'. 'Oh,' said Miss Willis, somewhat deflated. Miss Peebles glanced over to Miss Willis' effort and was confronted with an arrangement almost identical to hers, except that it had no deer. This time it was Miss Peebles who was annoyed. 'You can't copy mine,' said Miss Peebles, '*mine* is unique.' '*Mine*', said Miss Willis, 'is called "On Jordan's Bank" and I'm not going to change it.' Old Tom wandered past whistling 'Fight the Good Fight'. Miss Peebles trotted off to find an arbitrator.

Mrs Bulmer had artistically arranged a beautiful pedestal arrangement and Mr Bulmer propped a broom handle up beside it. The title read, 'My Faith it is an Oaken Staff'. Miss Peebles returned with Miss Dunn. 'They do look alike,' commented Miss Dunn as she stood in judgement over the contending flower displays, 'but I think as Miss Peebles's arrangement has the added interest of the deer we'll leave hers and turn yours into something else,' she finished, looking at Jordan's Bank. Miss Willis was furious; in a moment of anger she uprooted her flowers and threw the moss back into a bag. Tom wandered past again, this time singing 'Not What These Hands Have Done, Can Save This Guilty Soul'. That did it. Miss Willis stormed out of the church.

Pretty Miss Armitage had been quietly busy in a corner. She was totally smitten with Jeremy Lightfoot and followed him everywhere like a faithful dog. Unfortunately, Jeremy appeared not to notice the affectionate advances of Miss Armitage, so she remained unmarried and worked as a teacher. She had made a collage of a whale out of lentils and silver paper. In front she had placed the figure of a man made out of tiny flowers and the caption read 'Out of the Deep I Call'.

There was now a series of explosive noises coming from somewhere in the church. It turned out to be Mr Newington who was sneezing violently and uncontrollably into a large, white handkerchief. 'Pollen,' he sniffed, when Miss Foggerty asked if he was alright. 'I'm allergic to – to – tttttttaschoooo!' Miss Foggerty took a few paces backwards. 'To grasses,' finished Mr Newington, pointing to a large arrangement of wild grasses. Old Tom chose this moment to walk past, this time whistling 'Rescue the Perishing'.

Mrs Pettigrew found time between writing labels to portray the hymn 'Love Divine'. She filled a rosebowl with red roses and asparagus fern and placed it on the altar. Miss Willis returned carrying three pillows. Straight as a ramrod and with lips tightly pursed together, she worked in stony silence; no one liked to inquire what it was going to be. People cast sidelong glances at her while she worked but no one could work out what it was. Miss Willis piled the pillows on top of each other, then emptied out a large bag of cotton wool. 'Hope it's not supposed to be another icy mountain,' commented Miss Peebles to Miss Venables. Miss Willis was being most particular with the cotton wool; she fluffed it out, then pressed it over the pillows. This completed, she arranged some pink and white sweet-peas in vases and placed them on either side of the cotton-wool construction. Just at that moment everyone's attention was diverted. A loud clanking could be heard coming from the porch. 'Sounds like the ghost of Christmas past,' said Miss Dunn. With that, Old Tom entered the church dragging with him a large, rusty, ship's anchor on an equally rusty length of chain. He managed to get it as far as the hymn-book table, then he let it fall to the ground with a crash. How Old Tom came to be in possession of a ship's anchor, no one knew, and no one ever found out. Old Tom had spent all his working life on a farm.

Tom was now being helped by four tittering spinsters, Miss Venables, Miss Peebles and the two Miss Jameses. Scissors were busily snipping flowers and the stalks were flying in all directions, while water was being poured into vases and over the floor. Chicken-wire littered the hymn-book table. Vast quantities of greenery were eaten up by the arrangement. Miss Venables produced a length of pink ribbon and with a flourish she completed the display. Old Tom then proudly pinned up his parchment label which read 'Will Your Anchor Hold?' The rusty ship's anchor had been transformed and they all stood back to admire the effect. It was now a profusion of pink and white blooms, with a large pink bow completing the picture. Even Miss Dunn had to agree that it was a worthy effort. 'Will Your Anchor Hold?' faced Miss Birch's 'Rock of Ages' making a most impressive entrance to the flower festival.

Miss Willis packed up her belongings and left the church without speaking to anybody. One and all then rushed over to her arrangement to see what it was. On top of the pillows and cotton wool was a china dove and a single white rose. The title read, 'Lo! He Comes with Clouds Descending'.

All the arrangements were now complete. The church looked very beautiful. Miss Peebles glanced at Miss Venables and quoted, 'Art Thou Weary, Art Thou Languid?' Miss Venables said she was and suggested they went home for tea. Other parishioners soon followed their example and Mr Bulmer prepared to lock up. Miss Dunn was last to leave; she dusted her hands together, looked round the church, appeared satisfied and said, 'The Strife is O'er, the Battle Done', and strode out of the church. Mr Bulmer turned the key in the lock singing, 'The Day is Past and Over'. 'And just as well,' he muttered to himself, and he breathed deeply and went home for his tea.

The next morning Mr Bulmer and the curate arrived at the church at half-past nine to check that everything was in order. There was to be no entrance fee, but a collection plate was put in a prominent position by the door.

Mr Turner arrived and switched on his kindly light, which very kindly stayed on for a full twenty minutes until ten minutes past ten, when the first visitor arrived, then it inconsiderately went out. Old Tom arrived on cue whistling 'Give Me Oil in my Lamp, Keep me Burning', which did nothing to improve Mr Turner's temper.

Mr Bulmer's faith had taken a downward plunge during the night; his oaken staff lay at the foot of the flower arrangement. He righted his staff and then took up his place near the door – and the collection plate!

Jeremy arrived and minced over to view his flower arrangement. He looked at it critically, then moved the love-in-a-mist just the teeniest bit to the left. He watered it liberally with his mist sprayer and smoothed a crease out of the red velvet.

There was a steady trickle of visitors during the morning but the real rush was expected sometime after lunch. Organ music was to be played throughout the afternoon. Miss Proctor was going to play until three o'clock when Miss Venables would take over for twenty minutes to give her a tea break.

At two o'clock the expected rush arrived. They filed round the church viewing the various arrangements. Mr Bulmer had suggested charging an entrance fee but was out-voted by the rest of the committee. The next best thing he could do was to sit near the collection plate. Each visitor who left the church was treated to a pointed look from Mr Bulmer who then coughed loudly and nudged the collection plate. It worked, most of the time. Miss Venables arrived with her two brothers and their families. First they had to inspect 'All Creatures of our God and King' and admire the odd collection of animals and say nice things about it. Roger and Stephen took their father to see the Sunday school's effort. 'I trod in the pansies,' Stephen proudly told his father. 'Look, like this,' he said giving a demonstration. To everyone's horror, over went the pansies and water trickled off the font and made a dark stain on the floor. Fortunately it missed Mrs Pettigrew's label this time. Stephen's father stuffed the pansies back in the bowl and hoped that no one would notice.

Miss Willis arrived and parked herself in a pew near her arrangement so that she could listen to people's comments about it. It is said that listeners rarely hear good of themselves. The first comment Miss Willis heard was from a large lady who said to her friend, 'I don't know what a snow-covered field with a poor dead bird in it has to do with "Lo! He Comes With Clouds Descending"'. Miss Willis was about to leap up and explain when she realized she had no wish to be associated with what a tall gentleman was now referring to as 'free expression'.

Miss Proctor played softly on the organ. The soothing, gentle background music created an atmosphere of tranquillity in the flower-filled church. At three o'clock Miss Proctor handed over to Miss Venables. Miss Venables was an accomplished pianist but was not so familiar with the organ. However, she pushed back the stops Miss Proctor had been using and selected a few of her own. She liked the idea of the one marked 'trumpet' and pulled it out. Then she settled herself down, closed her eyes and thought about flowers, the summer-time and picnics in the country. Her fingers poised over the keys and she started to play. The atmosphere in the church changed abruptly as the merry tones of 'Teddybears' Picnic' echoed round the church with the voice of a trumpet. The vicar looked heavenwards and said, 'Dear me, oh dear, dear, me'. Miss Dunn apologized to a group of visitors and rushed off to put an end to Miss Venables' exuberant playing. There was a silent interval of ten minutes while Miss Proctor finished her tea and then the mellow tones of Handel once more filled the air. Visitors continued to pour in through the door during the rest of the afternoon. Most of the comments were favourable and the collection plate filled up nicely.

Miss Venables took her relations home for tea. Jeremy popped back into the church to give 'Hark the Glad Sound' one more spray. Miss Armitage also came into the church to stick back a few lentils which had dropped off her whale. 'Jeremy,' she called. 'Oh, hello,' replied Jeremy, 'do you think I need just the teeniest bit more asparagus fern in that corner?' he asked, tilting his head to one side. 'No,' answered Miss Armitage, 'I think it's wonderful just like that,' and she gazed adoringly at Jeremy. Jeremy didn't notice.

Miss Dunn could be heard giving her orders at the back of the church. 'Someone ought to sweep up the flower petals that have fallen,' she was saying. Then she spotted Miss Peebles and went and dragged her over to the Sunday school arrangement. 'Do you think you could do something about those pansies, they look dead to me,' said Miss Dunn. Miss Peebles looked at the wilted flowers in surprise. On closer inspection she saw that there was no water in the container, although she distinctly remembered re-filling the bowl after the morning's accident. 'It doesn't make a good impression if the flowers are dead,' continued Miss Dunn; 'it's bad enough having to put up with Mr Newington's "Thou to Whom the Sick and Dying"!' Miss Dunn had not approved of Mr Newington's choice of hymn but as the Vicar had been greatly impressed by what he referred to as the arrangement's surrealistic qualities she had felt compelled to allow it to stay.

Miss Dunn marched off to find something else to find fault with. Miss Peebles was slightly annoyed at the insinuation that she had purposely and wilfully neglected her pansies and did not feel inclined to walk all the way down to the kitchen to fetch water with which to fill up the bowl. As soon as Miss Dunn's back was turned, Miss Peebles lifted the lid off the font and scooped out a bowl of holy water, thrust the wilting pansies in it and went home for tea.

By five o'clock, most of the visitors had left. Mr Bulmer took the collection plate into the vestry and Mr Mitchell swept up the sand round the 'Rock of Ages'. The draught from the door had created a minor sandstorm at one point in the afternoon and the desert had spread towards the nave.

The church had now emptied completely leaving only the vicar seated amidst his congregation of flowers. He sat in a front pew between 'Hark the Glad Sound' and a bunch of Euphorbia. He sipped a cup of tea and hummed 'The Day Thou Gavest Lord is Ended'. The heavy perfume of a thousand flowers filled the church and silence descended.

The Slide Show

From time to time the vicar felt it incumbent on him to show an interest in the mission field and this he usually did by inviting Miss Armitage and the Miss Jameses to tea at the vicarage. I heard all about the latest teaparty from Miss Armitage one Wednesday afternoon when my mother and I had to wait for three-quarters of an hour at a windy bus stop after a visit to the dentist. Miss Birch spluttered past on her moped calling out a robust greeting. Miss Armitage and I giggled. Hilary Birch had acquired this mode of transport in the early summer and now she and her crash helmet were inseparable. Miss Armitage held tight to her woolly hat and in between gusts she told us that the Vicar had decided to hold a slide evening . . .

The idea had occurred to the vicar during tea. Mrs vicar had just passed the strawberry jam to one of the Miss Jameses. Miss James spread it over a slice of wholemeal bread and commented, 'This was one of the things I missed most when I was at the Zambezi Mission – a real English tea.' Her sister agreed and said what a joy it now was to be able to make a pot of tea with clean water instead of with the muddy liquid they'd had to haul out of a deep well in a rusty bucket. The vicar's eyebrows shot up and he looked horrified; he couldn't think of anything worse than not being able to have a decent cup of tea when one felt like it. Automatically he proffered his teacup to his wife, who automatically refilled it.

The Miss Jameses were now tucking into wholemeal scones in a genteel fashion and discussing the price of butter with Mrs vicar. The vicar was silent, brooding on the deprivations of missionary life. While the ladies had their mouths full of jam and scones, the vicar took the opportunity to ask,

'Didn't the mud clog up the tea strainer?' The Miss Jameses swallowed their scones and answered in unison, 'We didn't have the luxury of a strainer.' Edith explained that they had boiled up the tea in a battered old kettle, over an open fire. 'What, no teapot?' expostulated the vicar, removing the woolly tea-cosy and gazing fondly at the elegant bone-china teapot underneath. He thought of the comfortable brown china teapot they used in the kitchen and the small, individual teapot his wife had given him as a Christmas present and his heart went out to the Zambezi Mission. 'Those poor natives,' he muttered, 'no teapots!' 'I shouldn't worry,' said down to earth Edith James, 'they spend most of their time getting drunk on a home-brewed beer.' The vicar, looking very concerned, replied, 'Maybe if we sent out a quantity of tea and teapots, the natives would change from their alcoholic habits.' The sisters exchanged glances. They were very fond of their dear vicar but there were times when his remoteness from real life was exasperating. 'I'm afraid, Vicar', said Edith, 'that they would either sell the teapots at exorbitant prices to any visiting foreigners, or treat them as sacred ornaments – and they would probably ferment the tea-leaves into a potent alcoholic drink.' 'I remember that, as a young missionary, I was out in Indonesia', mused her sister, 'and there the natives chewed cassava; then they spat it out into huge bowls and left it to ferment.' Mrs vicar hurriedly excused herself and hastened to the kitchen to make a fresh pot of tea, while the vicar felt that Monday's tapioca pudding would never be the same again.

The vicar chewed on a slice of malt loaf then said, 'Isn't there anything we can do to help them?' To be up the Zambezi without a teapot was beyond the vicar's comprehension. Edith answered him saying, 'It would be nice if we could do something to help the Missionaries out there, it's a hard life.' 'They would appreciate a few pounds of tea,' put in Emily, 'but I should leave out the teapots, they'd only get broken in transit.' Edith looked round the vicar's homely dining-room. She realized that he had no idea of life on the Mission field. The vicar had gone to a comfortable upper-crust theological college, where he had dipped into obscure bible passages, acquired a knowledge of obsolete Latin phrases, perfected the art of nasal monotone delivery, mastered the basics of a three-point sermon and, thus qualified, was let loose into the church. It was time, thought Edith, to broaden the vicar's education. She spoke to her sister; 'Haven't we got some photographs somewhere of the Mission?' Emily said that they had a large box of slides. Thus the idea of a slide show was born. It was decided to charge an entry fee and the proceeds would be used to buy useful items to send to the gallant sisters up the Zambezi.

Like most ideas it snowballed. For the first half of the evening, the Parish would see slides of the Mission, but after refreshments they were to be given the privilege of seeing slides of Miss Birch's holiday in Switzerland, followed by The Scouts' Annual Camp by Jeremy and, if time allowed, Miss Whittick's long weekend in Bournemouth. There was some doubt as to whether the latter would turn up in time for the show. Church Secretary, Ethel Whitticks, was late for everything. She always looked as if she had just fought her way against a force ten gale. Her hair was normally awry and she usually had straw or sawdust adhering to her person. Miss Whitticks, when she was not scribbling down useless information in the PCC minute book, spent most of her time at home with a menagerie of furred and feathered friends.

Within a month, the night of the slide show had arrived. Edith James peered into the hall mirror to adjust her hat and called out to her sister, 'Have you got the slides, dear?' In reply Emily came out into the hall and placed a large box of slides by the front door, all ready for when the Major came to collect it. The two sisters had spent the last fortnight sorting through their slides, arranging them in a logical order and making certain they were all the right way up, ready to go straight into the projector. Edith went to check that the back door was locked, leaving the hall mirror free for Emily to make the final adjustments to *her* hat. The loud toot-a-toot-toot of a car horn heralded the arrival of the Major and the slide projector. Emily gave her hat a final tweak and rushed to the front door to open it. In her haste she tripped over an ornately carved, Victorian hatstand and landed, rather ungainly, in a terracotta pot already occupied by a flourishing Maidenhair fern. There was a loud knock on the front door. Edith, hurrying to see why Emily had not admitted the Major, skidded on a slip-mat and flew towards the front door. To a cry of 'I've told you not to polish under the mats!' Edith collided with an umbrella stand and landed on top of the box of slides by the front door. The impact of Edith James on a cardboard box full of slides was similar to a supernova explosion. The box was flattened and the carefully arranged slides scattered across the hall floor like meteorites.

A moustache appeared at the letter box. 'Are you alright in there?' boomed the Major; 'thought I heard a bit of a crash.' Emily disengaged herself from the clutches of the Maidenhair fern and emerged from the confines of the terracotta pot, brushing John Innes No. 3 off her overcoat. 'Just coming, Major,' she called. She undid the two large bolts on the front door and was able to open it far enough to admit the Major's head. Her sister was effectively acting as a human doorstop. Edith was sitting on the prickly door-mat, rubbing her shins and looking aghast at the slides, once so carefully arranged in the box, now so casually strewn the length of the hall.

Some five minutes later, the Major had pacified the Miss Jameses, gathered up the slides and deposited them all in the back of the car. 'Soon sort 'em out once we get to the church hall,' he said encouragingly, and with that he turned the key in the ignition and they were off.

There was considerable activity in the hall when they arrived. Mr Bulmer was setting out rows of chairs, Mr Rushmore the Church Treasurer, was counting loose change into a rusty Oxo tin and the vicar was attempting to assist Mr Newington in fixing up the projection screen. A crash of crockery in the kitchen announced the presence of Miss Dunn.

The Miss Jameses, as ex-missionaries of the Zambezi Mission, were not given to panicking, but they came very near to it as they assessed the disorder in the slide box. They had half-an-hour in which to sort slides which had previously taken two weeks to put in order. The spluttering of a motorbike engine and a generous waft of exhaust fumes through the open door meant that Miss Birch had arrived. She was wearing her best tweed two-piece and her brogues for the occasion. With her crash helmet still strapped to her head, she made her entry carrying a box of slides, a large Gruyère cheese and a cuckoo clock, the pendulum of which gave Mr Rushmore a hearty bash on the knuckles as she stomped past. 'It's me effects,' announced Miss Birch. 'Thought it would add authenticity to me slides, give folks a flavour of life in foreign climes and all that.' She deposited cheese, cuckoo clock and crash helmet on top of the piano. 'Got any effects?' breathed Miss Birch heartily to the two Miss Jameses who were kneeling on the floor surrounded by slides. Edith's patience was beginning to evaporate and she rather snapped an answer to Miss Birch. 'Apart from a test-tube of Zambezi water, filled with mosquito larvae, worms, tsetse-fly grubs and bilharzia, no we haven't!'

Unfortunately, Mr Newington overheard this comment and his imagination immediately ran riot. He beat a hasty retreat to the vestry where he donned a pair of pink rubber gloves kindly left by Mrs Twigg the church cleaner. He found an economy-sized bottle of disinfectant and unearthed a pair of old underpants, previously the property of Mr Twigg and currently used by Mrs Twigg to polish the brasses. Thus equipped, Mr Newington re-emerged into the hall, bumping into Jeremy who had just arrived with his box of slides. Jeremy gave a gasp as he was confronted by an apparition wearing pink gloves and waving a pair of ancient underpants. Jeremy had to sit down. Mr Newington's face then appeared from behind the economy-sized bottle of disinfectant and he confided in Jeremy that the Miss Jameses had only gone and brought bilharzia with them and wasn't it dreadful. 'Oh,' replied Jeremy, 'you must introduce me to him,' and he looked round to make the acquaintance of Bill whoever-he-was. 'No, no,' said an agitated Mr Newington, 'it's a tropical disease!' Now it was Jeremy's turn to look alarmed. He replied by saying, 'Mother would never have let me come tonight if she'd known. I'm delicate you know,' he added by way of explanation. Jeremy was in fact only delicate in his imagination. The vicar, who was waiting for Mr Newington to help him fix up the projector, now came over to the vestry to inquire if everything was all right. He received a rather garbled account of the situation from Jeremy and, looking slightly disturbed, the vicar hurried over to Edith James.

Taking her by the arm and leading her to a quiet corner, he whispered confidentially, 'I'm rather concerned about your test tubes full of tropical water and the – er – accompanying diseases; only one can't be too careful – there will be tea and biscuits about later and . . .' Miss James looked him straight in the eye and said, 'It was a joke, Vicar.' 'Oh, I see,' said the vicar, not really understanding at all, 'a joke, splendid, jolly good,' and he hurried back to Jeremy and Mr Newington with the glad tidings.

The Major was attempting to plug in the projector. This was not as easy as it would seem. The only socket available was situated in the kitchen. The Major wired up an extension lead but it posed a safety hazard as it lay draped over chairs and running along the floor. He decided not to plug in until everyone was safely seated.

The audience were beginning to arrive. Mr Rushmore collected sixpences at the door. Miss Venables arrived together with Miss Peebles and Miss Willis. Hilary Birch noting their arrival stomped over and collared Miss Venables. 'I wonder', she barked, 'if you could play me some music to help with me effects.'

Seeing Miss Venables' uncomprehending gaze, she continued, 'I thought "The Happy Wanderer" would be appropriate, if you could start playing that as soon as the slide of me striding along a mountain path comes up.' Miss Venables professed herself delighted at the idea and then settled herself down next to Miss Peebles to await the first part of the slide show. Miss Peebles craned her neck to see who had turned up for the occasion. She noted that Mrs Turner and Mrs Pettigrew were seated a few rows behind and that Miss Armitage was sitting demurely at the end of a row holding Jeremy's slide notes. Craning her neck still further she saw the vicar's wife arrive with the Reverend Sydney Poddlewell. Miss Proctor' who was hunched into a seat in the back row with her handbag clasped on her lap, shrank into her raincoat still further. She had memories of the Reverend Poddlewell and the summer picnic which were still vivid in her memory, but that, as they say, is another story.

The Reverend Poddlewell, who was by nature an outgoing sort of chap, noticed Miss Proctor and going over to her he clamped a hand on her shoulder and said, 'Why, it's Miss Proctor I believe; how are you?' Miss Proctor felt the colour rush to her face. The extrovert had captured the introvert and Miss Proctor went to pieces. Trying to cover up her feeling of inadequacy and attempting to emulate Mr Poddlewell's friendly greeting and so deceive him into thinking she too was a social creature, she responded without thinking by saying, 'Hello, *Sydney.*' No sooner was his name out of her mouth than Miss Proctor wished the floor would open up and swallow her. She had been over-familiar with a Reverend Gentleman. She spent the rest of the evening worrying about it. The Reverend Poddlewell quite sensibly spent the evening enjoying the slide show.

Miss Whitticks arrived, as was to be expected, at the very last minute. Her excuse this time was that the tortoise had woken up and tried to clamber out of his hibernation box, added to which the guinea pig and the rabbit had quarrelled over a carrot at tea-time and Miss Whitticks had had to restore order in the hutch. Miss Whitticks was accompanied as usual by a collection of relations. As well as the cousin who smelt of horses and the one who smelt of dogs and the brother who was a farmer, she had also brought along a sister who smelt of pig farms and a second cousin who smelt of pigeons. She also introduced Miss Peebles to a brother who kept a wet-fish shop. From where Miss Peebles sat she suspected there was probably a dead haddock in his pocket. For once Miss Peebles was grateful for the overpowering aroma of Miss Willis' mothballs as it counteracted the odour of gone-off fish. Fortunately the whole family decided to move nearer the front and Miss Venables was able to return her smelling salts to her handbag.

Mr Newington and the vicar had, after numerous attempts, succeeded in setting up the slide screen. The hall doors were now closed, and Miss Dunn had abandoned the tea-urn, a sure sign that the entertainment was about to commence.

There was a deep, throaty, roar as the projector burst into life and a shaft of light illuminated the heads of all those in the front row. 'I think the screen needs to be a bit higher,' said the Major. Mr Newington and the vicar stumbled towards the front, the vicar apologizing as he accidentally trod on the corns of several parishioners. The two men raised the screen a little higher and now only Mr Bulmer's head cast a silhouette on the screen. 'Bit higher!' shouted the Major. The vicar, attempting to oblige, released a screw and the whole screen folded up on itself. The beam of light now illuminated an ancient radiator which was immediately behind the screen. The two men stood the screen up once more and returned it to its previous position. It was decided that it was safer to move Mr Bulmer than to coerce the screen to greater heights. Consequently, Mr Bulmer retired to a side seat.

The two Miss Jameses sat next to the Major and kept their fingers crossed that the slides would all be the right way up. The last dozen or so had been packed into the slide box with even more haste than the rest. Edith prepared to deliver her commentary. The opening slide depicting a group of mud huts with thatched roofs brought a ripple of interest from the audience, and the slides of the Zambezi Mission got underway. Half-way through Emily began to relax, the slides had all appeared the right way up except for a few which had been back-to-front, but this had not been noticeable. There were views of the mission hospital, showing rows of low beds covered in brilliant white linen with grateful patients reclining on them. There were little children with ebony faces and huge eyes playing with a ball at the mission school. There were pictures of the clinics which were held in outlying districts. The sight of one of the Miss Jameses with a hypodermic made Mr Newington feel a little queasy but it was not long before the slide changed to one of the parched fields surrounding the mission. The slide following this, however, was a disaster. It revealed an upside-down Edith astride an upside-down bicycle and it caused much laughter. The Major hastily switched to the next slide, which depicted a back-to-front sideways-on view of Emily talking to a tribal chief.

From then on things went from bad to worse. A slide showing Edith, the right way up, came into view, but it was of Edith dressed in an archaic bathing costume. Edith was glad of the darkness; it covered her embarrassment. 'However did that one get in?' hissed Edith to Emily. Before Emily could reply, the next slide came into focus depicting Emily covered from head to foot in mud. 'That was the day you had an argument with an ox,' whispered Edith. 'I know,' said Emily, 'and the ox won.' It was at this point that Miss Dunn received a telepathic message from the tea-urn saying it had reached boiling point and she jumped up from her seat and made her way towards the kitchen. It was bound to happen sooner or later – she tripped over the projector lead plunging the hall into darkness. Fortunately, Miss Dunn only suffered minor abrasions to her pride, and the Miss Jameses felt it was a heaven-sent answer ending their ignominy on the screen.

Over the next twenty minutes, cups of tea were dispensed and biscuits consumed. Mr Newington bit too hard on a ginger-nut and lost a small piece of filling, but apart from that the refreshments passed without incident. While Miss Dunn supervised the collection of empty teacups and the vicar squeezed the final dregs from the large enamel teapot, Jeremy got his slides ready. Miss Armitage moved her chair a little closer to Jeremy and waited for the lights to go out. 'Right-Oh, everyone,' the Major boomed, 'second half!' There was a general murmur of anticipation; the projector whirred and the lights were turned off. For the next twenty minutes the parish were treated to Jeremy's slides of the Scout summer camp. As each slide went up Miss Armitage gave a little sigh of appreciation. The Scout camp had been transformed from a collection of dingy tents and grubby little boys to artistically focused images. Only Jeremy could have taken a photograph of a back-lit latrine, the sun sparkling off a tent peg and an unpricked sausage exploding over the camp fire. The angles used by Jeremy to take the transparencies were an art form in themselves. One shot was taken by hanging over a rock crevice. Miss Armitage gripped her chair. Jeremy explained that this was the day Stephen had lost his woggle. It later turned up stuck in a blackberry bush but at the time the photograph was taken it was thought that the woggle had ended its days in a ravine. Jeremy was in the process of describing one particular slide on the screen (it was of a fairy ring at twilight) when suddenly a loud 'Cuckoo!' rang out through the hall. Miss Birch's cuckoo clock had decided to strike the hour. Miss Peebles nearly came off her chair with shock.

'I say, frightfully sorry everyone!' shouted Miss Birch, as she attempted to quell the raucous cuckoo by stuffing her woollen muffler over the door in the clock. It had little effect; the bird burst through shrieking, 'Cuckoo, cuckoo!' It was nine o'clock and the bird was determined to announce every one of the hours. When it had cuckooed the ninth and final hour, the bird withdrew into the clock, slamming his door defiantly behind him. Miss Birch apologized again and Jeremy was allowed to continue, with a slide of the camp fire. At the first cuckoo, Jeremy had clutched Miss Armitage with shock and, to her eternal delight, his hand still rested on hers in the darkness. Jeremy was of course unaware of the fact that Miss Armitage's pulse rate was doing ninety and calmly went on with his commentary. He was also unaware that his hand rested on Miss Armitage's. Jeremy's slides came to an end, there was a rapturous round of applause and Miss Armitage sighed as Jeremy removed his hand to gather up his notes.

'Are you ready?' hissed Miss Birch to Miss Venables, 'I'm on next.' Miss Venables made her way to the piano, Mr Bartholomew kindly lighting her way with his pocket torch. 'Right, everyone ready?' shouted Miss Birch. Old Tom turned his hearing-aid down. The opening slide revealed a mountain-side covered with wild flowers and Miss Venables prepared herself for her part on the piano. She hadn't long to wait. The next slide showed Miss Birch striding along a mountain path. Miss Venables let loose on the keyboard with 'The Happy Wanderer'. When Miss Birch was able to get a word in between bars she said, 'Friend of mine took the photograph, name of Herr Gruber.' Before anyone had a chance to envisage any romantic attachments, the next slide showed Frau Gruber and all the little Grubers. There was an out-of-focus cow on the following slide. 'Bloomin' cow bells kept me awake all night' informed Miss Birch. Miss Venables rippled a few tinkling notes in imitation of cow bells. 'Next slide please, Major,' commanded Miss Birch. The Major tutted in his moustache; the next slide was jammed in the projector. 'There's a bit of a technical hitch,' he whispered to Miss Birch, 'can you keep talking?' Miss Birch kept talking. She told a long boring anecdote about Herr Gruber and a cow bell. Miss Peebles yawned, Old Tom nodded and Miss Willis wished she'd brought a cushion – the hard hall chair was numbing her nether regions. The Major borrowed a hair pin from Mrs Pettigrew and was able to free the errant slide and he quickly slotted the next one in. The interest of the audience was immediately regained. The slide was of Herr Gruber blowing an enormous alpine horn. Miss Venables couldn't resist it. She put her foot on the loud pedal and struck a few bass discords. It was too much for the Gruyère cheese seated on top of the piano; the vibrations sent it rolling to the edge, it plummeted from the stage, bounced past a surprised curate and rolled like ball-lightning towards the vicar. It crashed into the vicar's chair, rebounded, and shot down the aisle between the chairs. Gaining momentum, it hurtled past the Reverend Poddlewell, ran over Miss Willis' foot, cannoned into Miss Dunn's handbag and finally came to rest under a radiator. 'That didn't do me cheese much good,' barked Miss Birch. It had not done much for Miss Willis's bunion either. Miss Birch hastened down the aisle to inspect her Gruyère for dents.

Meanwhile, the Major continued showing the slides. There was one of a beer garden showing Miss Birch dressed in khaki shorts and long woollen walking socks, offset by a pair of stout boots. Herr Gruber was dressed much the same and both appeared to be downing pints of beer. Scenes of snow-topped mountains, blue skies and wild flowers completed Miss Birch's set of slides. Miss Birch's commentary had ceased while she rescued the Gruyère and Miss Venables had filled the silence by playing suitable music. The audience had been treated to two verses of 'All Things Bright and Beautiful', half-a-dozen bars from Beethoven's Pastoral Symphony and the whole of Miss Venables' favourite, 'The Venetian Boat Song' – geography had never been her strong point. The final slide showed Miss Birch, map in hand, rucksack on her back, striding purposefully down a steep mountain track.

Miss Venables threw herself straight into 'She'll be Coming Round the Mountain When She Comes'. The audience broke into spontaneous applause.

It was the Major who started the singing and he was closely followed by Jeremy, to whom the song brought back happy memories of the Scout camp fire. Soon there was hearty singing and clapping. This acted like a drug on Miss Venables and her playing became louder and even more enthusiastic. Miss Birch's crash helmet succumbed to the vibrations and threw itself to the floor. Miss Peebles remembered her adolescent years in the Girl Guides and with memories of smoky sausages and sparks flying she sang along with the others. Miss Willis felt uncomfortable; the behaviour which was going on around her was completely alien to her nature and she rather wished she was somewhere else. Miss Proctor was moved by the war-time spirit which seemed to have pervaded the hall and she wiped a tear from the corner of her eye. Like many introverts she always observed from the periphery, but it was never a detached observation; she experienced emotions more acutely than those actively involved.

Miss Birch, clutching the Gruyère cheese to her bosom, thus defying it to escape ever again, made her way up the aisle in time to the music, greatly pleased with the audience reaction to her slide show. Miss Peebles' gaze followed Miss Birch as she made her way to the back of the hall. She saw Miss Venables, who was lit by a faint light from the kitchen; she had her head thrown back and was singing lustily; her face was flushed and her eyes were sparkling. She was beginning to bounce on the piano stool; Miss Peebles knew the signs – her friend was becoming over-excited. Miss Peebles stopped singing and wondered how to put an end to Miss Venables' playing before an 'incident' occurred, which it usually did when Miss Venables became over-enthusiastic.

Fortunately, Miss Birch had now arrived at the back of the hall and announced that her slides were finished and Miss Peebles breathed a sigh of relief as Miss Venables' playing came to a triumphant conclusion. The Major switched off the projector and the main lights went on. The singing stopped instantly. The British inhibitions had been shed in the darkness, but with the advent of bright light the parishioners felt themselves uncovered and they looked at the floor with embarrassment, shuffled their feet and avoided looking at one another. Miss Willis gave a sigh of relief; things were back to normal. The ensuing silence was broken only by the extremely loud gurglings and hiccuping of prehistoric plumbing as the vicar pulled the chain in the choir vestry toilet. His wife wished she was invisible.

The Whitticks contingent in the front row sat up expectantly. Ethel Whitticks handed the Major her box of slides and the lights went out. The audience settled themselves as a picture of Bournemouth seafront came into view. Miss Whitticks could just be seen, standing by a corporation dustcart in the corner. Miss Whitticks took up the commentary with the next slide. 'This is me,' she said, 'standing on the steps of the hotel.' The next slide showed her standing outside the door of the hotel; this was followed by Miss Whitticks standing in front of a hydrangea bush, at a side entrance to the hotel. The hydrangea appeared to have been affected by winter gales and sea salt and it looked in a state of collapse. However, Ethel Whitticks stood out well, wearing a white woollen cardigan and a red hat. This was followed by one of

Miss Whitticks on the pier. Next came Miss Whitticks outside the hotel again, followed by Miss Whitticks in a deck chair on the prom. This showed a close-up of her knees and a large white handbag. The next two slides depicted Miss Whitticks leaning on the promenade rail looking out to sea, and one of her looking towards the camera with her back to the sea. Another slide showed only the top of Miss Whitticks' head and a quantity of blue sky, while another depicted Miss Whitticks' white sling-backs and a quantity of green grass.

It seemed to Miss Whitticks that the Major was not leaving the slides on the screen for very long. In fact, it could almost be said that he was rushing it! The Major had seen just how many slides there were to get through and he had rather hoped to be home before midnight. The audience saw Miss Whitticks in a deckchair in the hotel garden, Miss Whitticks in a green dress outside a coffee shop and Miss Whitticks in a blue dress outside a tea shop, with Woolworth's on the left. Miss Peebles instantly sat up and took notice. After this came a picture of Miss Whitticks wearing a cream hat, with a telegraph pole through her head. The Major was getting desperate and began a frenzied attempt to whizz the slides through as fast as they would go, the haste of which surpassed all the decency of English manners. The audience viewed Miss Whitticks wearing a yellow dress, blue dress, pink dress, green dress, an overcoat, raincoat, half-coat and jumper. They saw her drinking hot tea, iced coffee, orange juice and gin, eating ice-cream, cheese rolls, scones and strawberry jam. She wore a blue hat, headscarf, sun-hat, rain-hat; they saw her outside a restaurant, gift shop and swimming pool on a fine day, a wet day, wind'll-blow-your-hat-off-day. Miss

Whitticks came in focus and out of focus, natural and unnatural. She was laughing, frowning, smiling and grimacing. The projector had finally had enough of Miss Whitticks and the light-bulb blew. The image of Miss Whitticks was removed from the screen in an instant. Miss Birch's cuckoo clock decided it was time to announce the hour of eleven o'clock and Jeremy nearly choked on a humbug.

Someone switched on the lights and Miss Whitticks could be heard saying, 'Oh but what a shame, you haven't seen them all yet; you must come to tea and then we can go through them all at a more leisurely pace.' Miss Peebles took Miss Venables by the arm and manoeuvred her hastily to a side door. 'I think', she whispered to Miss Venables, 'that we should leave at once before we get issued with an invite.' Miss Venables agreed with alacrity and the two elderly ladies made their exit, undetected, through a side door. They tiptoed past the dustbins and disappeared into the night.

The Entertainment

The long, dark winter evenings had arrived and it was time to start rehearsals for the 'Entertainment'. A notice went up on the notice-board, which read, 'Anyone wishing to participate in the event should hand their names in to Mr Bulmer within the next two weeks.' An entertainments committee was set up and, once the names were in, the committee drew up a programme.

My mother and I knew all about entertainment. Most Saturday evenings we entertained the cat with musical renderings. The three of us would gather in the dining-room with the piano, while my father sought refuge as far away as possible. In the winter the storm-force winds would lift the carpet up from its linoleum surround and it would undulate like the sea. My mother barricaded us in with sausage-shaped door stops and pulled thick curtains over the door and windows. Crackers, the cat, would curl up unhygienically on the table and the concert would commence.

My mother's piano playing rivalled Miss Venables'. She had been much in demand on the Naafi piano during the war. One day, while home on leave, my mother had been playing the piano as Grandma knitted socks to send to her son out in Rangoon, when suddenly there was a terrific explosion. The Germans had dropped a bomb which landed several streets away. At that precise moment my mother was playing a popular tune of the day called 'If I Might Only Come to You'. Grandma continued knitting and simply said, 'Well we didn't mean it that literally!' However, I digress – back to our concert . . .

After a few excursions across the keys to warm up, we would select a song and then off we would go. This would be followed by a piano duet with my mother playing a complicated arrangement of her own invention while I tried to concentrate on fitting my notes in wherever there was time or space. We would both manage to hit the finale at the same time and the green glass vase on the piano top would vibrate excitedly. One great favourite was a song entitled, 'The King's Horses and the King's Men'. This contained a line referring to the Mayor riding in a coach and pair. My mother always changed this and sang 'Riding in an old armchair' and we would get the giggles at the thought of such a wonderful sight. This would be followed by a few gospel choruses with me playing the guitar. Then it would be time for our party piece which was 'The Holy City'. The sheet music was spotty-brown and crumbling. It had belonged to my great-great-grandfather. Softly we began the verse, then slowly the rumbling piano chords broke loose into a crescendo as my mother worked the loud pedal with her foot and we were catapulted into the chorus. Reaching the top notes with ease we loudly sang 'Jerusalem, Je-rooo-sa-lem'. When the cat stuffed his paws over his ears we would give him an encore. Oh yes, my mother and I knew all about entertainment.

However, for the purpose of the parish concert our musical talents remained untapped. Mother and her friend were involved with the Mothers' Union and they were responsible for doing the refreshments. I was to be part of the Guide performance. Several Guides had each been given a slot in the programme. Anna and I decided to perform 'Skimbleshanks the Railway Cat'. For this Anna dressed in a long black jumper, black tights and a balaclava helmet on to which we stuck black ears. I gave her whiskers and a black nose with an eyeliner pen. My part was to learn T. S. Eliot's poem off by heart so that I could stand on stage and recite while Anna pranced about being Skimbleshanks. Andrew Lloyd Webber would have been proud of us. It did dawn on me that Anna had the easier part.

Let us now take a look behind the scenes and see what the Parishioners made of the Entertainment . . .

REHEARSAL

It was inevitable that some people would be upset by the arrangements. Mr Newington was the first to experience rejection. He had asked to sing in the male quartet but was told it had been changed to a trio and therefore he was surplus to requirements. He offered to join the morris-dance team but found their numbers were already made up. In the end he suggested that he did a monologue but was politely informed that there was no room left on the programme. Mr Newington sensed there was something wrong but no one would tell him why he hadn't got a part. It was Miss Dunn who eventually told him. She was totally insensitive when it came to people's feelings and with an air of dismissal she told him, 'Well, its not surprising you're not on the programme; you're more than likely to be ill and that makes you unreliable.' Mr Newington was at first deeply hurt and passed through several days of melancholy. As that gradually receded he suddenly erupted in anger at the injustice of it all. He chose to erupt in the middle of a steak and kidney pie. Waving his knife and fork at his wife he shouted, 'Serve them right if they all get mumps!' He impaled a few peas on the end of his fork with intense feeling, then continued, 'I hope that they all get flu, and measles and laryngitis.' He cut through a carrot with venom, sending gravy over the tablecloth, but he still hadn't finished and growled, 'I hope the stage caves in and the scenery falls down,' and he savagely smashed a potato to emphasize his point. 'Now you're being ridiculous dear,' said his wife, taking his plate away and replacing it with a bowl of prunes and custard. Mrs Newington crossed her fingers and hoped that her husband wouldn't start throwing prune stones across the table, but Mr Newington was now feeling a little ashamed of himself and he meekly spooned up his prunes and custard. It was eventually decided that Mr Newington could be a stage hand assisting Mr Bulmer. He still practised his monologue in private just in case someone did go down with laryngitis on the night.

Miss Dunn had appointed herself as Director; this was not popular, but she was immovable once she'd made up her mind about something. The musicians were thankful that Miss Proctor had been chosen as Musical Director. The curate had been asked to compère the show and to introduce each act. His presence was not required at the first few rehearsals.

Miss Dunn ensconced herself on a wooden chair in front of the stage and shouted instructions. The show started with a musical item sung by the Wives' Group, and Miss Dunn let them off quite lightly. The vicar was on next. Miss Dunn was not intimidated by men of high position and he received his orders loud and clear. The vicar reminded himself that he must be charitable to those poor people who possessed an unfortunate manner and he did his best to respond to Miss Dunn's wishes. He had chosen to recite 'Home Thoughts From Abroad', the poem by Robert Browning. Clasping his hands together and looking upwards he began 'Oh, to be in England . . .' 'Stop!' shouted Miss Dunn. The vicar looked surprised; he was not aware that he had done anything wrong as yet. Miss Dunn continued, 'Please note the words are "Oh to be in *England*" not "Oh, to be in Heaven", Please look at the audience and not skywards.' The vicar obligingly lowered his gaze and began again. Miss Dunn made a few further adjustments and dismissed the vicar until the next rehearsal.

When he got home the vicar practised his poem in front of the bedroom mirror. He had not been aware till Miss Dunn pointed it out that he blinked as he recited, that his shoulders sagged, that his stomach stuck out and that his feet pointed in opposite directions. Gazing at his reflection, he drew in a deep breath, pulled in his stomach, pulled back his shoulders, adjusted his feet and stared unblinking like a stuffed cod into the mirror. In this position he opened his mouth wide, like Miss Dunn had told him; his resemblance to a fish increasing and, enunciating like a débutante taking elocution lessons, he began to recite. Fortunately his wife came in at that moment and put a stop to it. 'You'll be a laughing stock if you go on stage looking like that,' she told him. Relieved, the vicar breathed out and his body was allowed to fall back to its natural position. 'That woman', remarked his wife, 'is going to upset a lot of people before the performance is over. I just hope they don't all decide to go on strike.' The vicar's wife tried to feel charitable towards Miss Dunn, but it was difficult when every day she was confronted with a hideous cushion, made by Miss Dunn, that the vicar had won at a bring and buy sale. After the insulting way Miss Dunn had tried to re-model her husband, she now felt no qualms about removing the cushion from the vicarage and depositing it on a chair in the darkest corner of the church vestry. Reassured by his wife's comments that he looked perfectly normal and that she wouldn't want him any different, the vicar put on his pyjamas, climbed into bed and was soon fast asleep. And if he dreamt of Miss Dunn falling through a hole in the stage, that was his business.

Rehearsals continued every Thursday evening. Miss Peebles, Mrs Mitchell and Miss Granger were to be Gilbert and Sullivan's 'Three Little Maids from School'. Miss Granger had been an opera singer in her heyday but was now reduced to giving singing lessons to little girls whose doting mothers paid her exorbitant fees, convinced that dear Sarah or Amanda had the voice of an angel. Miss Granger could have told them otherwise but she was willing to put up with Sarah's off-key caterwauling for the sake of the fat fees paid out by the parents; it enabled her to continue in the manner to which she had been accustomed.

The three ladies had been having private rehearsals at Miss Granger's house and were almost note-perfect. Miss Peebles had tried to emulate Miss Granger's perfectly controlled soprano voice, but the effect had been reminiscent of a screech-owl. Miss Granger and Mrs Mitchell gently suggested to Miss Peebles that she sang a little quieter. Fortunately, Miss Peebles also had to learn a dance routine to accompany the song and her voice softened as she concentrated on moving her feet in the right direction.

Miss Foggerty and some willing helpers were responsible for costumes and make-up. The three little maids from school posed some problems, although the kimonos were easily made. Two were manufactured from some old vicarage curtains and looked quite attractive being patterned with sprays of forget-me-nots. The third was made from an old armchair cover donated by Miss Willis. It produced an unusual-looking kimono, being of a chintzy pattern, but it was the only other large piece of material available. The wigs were a problem. Miss Granger had a suitable one left from her opera days but Miss Peebles and Mrs Mitchell were more difficult to accommodate. Eventually, the friend of a friend of Mrs Phillips, who worked in a clothes shop, allowed them to borrow two wigs which belonged to the dummies in the window. They didn't look quite right, but as beggars couldn't be choosers Miss Dunn had to declare herself satisfied with them. Miss Venables provided three pairs of sock-knitting needles and these were poked into the wigs to give them more oriental authenticity.

Jeremy Lightfoot had, to Miss Armitage's delight, agreed to play a duet with her. Jeremy tinkled up and down the scale on his flute while Miss Armitage scraped away at the cello. Little Miss Proctor stood on an orange crate and conducted them with a twelve inch ruler. She was only conducting them at rehearsals; for the actual performance they were to be let loose on their own. 'Jeremy dear,' said Miss Proctor, 'you finished two bars ahead of Miss Armitage. I think we'll have to take it again from the beginning.' Once again Jeremy tinkled and trilled at the flute while Miss Armitage grated and scraped at the cello. Most of the time Miss Armitage gazed adoringly at Jeremy instead of at the music or Miss Proctor, and the result was less than perfect. This time Jeremy and Miss Armitage arrived at the end of the music together and Miss Proctor asked them to play their second piece. Half-way through, Miss Dunn, who had been sitting in front of the stage making copious notes, suddenly stood up and coughed loudly. Jeremy and Miss Armitage were oblivious of this. Jeremy was at one with his flute, transported on an arpeggio of notes; he was floating in a musical wonderland. Miss Armitage sawed away at the cello, lost not in her playing but in her vision of the flute-playing Jeremy. She saw him as a Greek Adonis. He had totally the wrong build and colouring for this, but Miss Armitage was not put off by such mere detail. She saw him standing in a sunlit olive grove with the sweet scent of myrtle on the air. Miss Dunn was annoyed that her loud coughing had not put an end to the music as she had intended, so she now clapped her hands loudly and shouted 'Stop!' Miss Proctor nearly fell off her orange crate with shock. Jeremy was suspended in mid-trill and Miss Armitage was forced to exchange her myrtle-scented olive grove for the less salubrious delights of the church hall. 'This piece of music doesn't sound right to me,' continued Miss Dunn. 'I think you're playing it in the wrong key and it's gone flat.' Jeremy and Miss Armitage blinked uncomprehendingly. They were both of a gentle and sensitive temperament and Miss Dunn's criticism had cut them to the quick. Miss Proctor who was herself normally timid and sensitive suddenly found herself defending her charges. She had watched Miss Dunn throughout previous rehearsals, dictating and ordering people about and had greatly disapproved. This time Miss Dunn had gone too far; she began to address Miss Proctor but found to her surprise that the worm had turned. Miss Proctor was seething inside with righteous anger. Looking Miss Dunn coolly in the eye she said, '*I* am the Musical Director and if there is any criticism to be made *I* am the one who will make it.' Miss Dunn was not used to being answered back and she started to raise her voice in reply, 'I tell you it's gone flat; it sounds dreadful.' Miss Proctor normally only thought of what she *might* have said to people after the event had passed but tonight she was running high on adrenalin and she became intoxicated with a sense of strength and power. She fairly screeched at Miss Dunn, 'I know a B flat from an F sharp when I hear one which is more than I can say for you!' Miss Proctor jumped off her orange crate, picked up her music case, flung her gabardine over her arm and marched out of the church hall. While Miss Dunn was recovering from the surprise, Jeremy and Miss Armitage took the opportunity to make a hasty departure into the wings. A buzz of excitement passed round the hall. Mousy Miss Proctor had done something they had all longed to do but had never dared – she had stood up to Miss Dunn.

The cold, frosty night air hit Miss Proctor like a whip. She suddenly felt shaky all over; her legs turned to jelly. After putting on her gabardine raincoat she sat down on a low stone wall by a laurel bush. 'Oh dear, what have I done?' she moaned to herself. Much time passed as Miss Proctor sat under the stars. The frosty air numbed her hands and feet, but she noticed neither. How long she might have sat there is anyone's guess but the curate had just locked up the vestry and was making his way home when he passed along the path near Miss Proctor. Seeing a dark, huddled figure sitting on the wall, he first thought that someone had been taken unwell, but as he drew closer he saw Miss Proctor gently rocking to and fro murmuring to herself. Hearing footsteps, Miss Proctor jumped up and, realizing that it was the curate, she rushed forwards. 'I've done something dreadful,' she confessed in a rush. Mr Crumpton's favourite panacea for distressed old ladies was a reassuring pat on the shoulder and a murmured 'I understand'. It worked as it always did, and soon Miss Proctor had stopped shaking and felt more in control of herself. They stood in silence for a short time, while the curate allowed Miss Proctor to compose herself; then he said, 'As I understand it, Miss Dunn may be the overall director but you as *Musical* Director are solely responsible for musical technicalities.' Mr Crumpton had heard various comments passed round the church recently, none of which were very complimentary to Miss Dunn, and he felt that now might be the time to sort something out before the whole performance was in jeopardy.

Miss Proctor's courage nearly failed when the curate asked her to go back to the rehearsal, but she mustered all her strength and followed the broad figure of Mr Crumpton back into the hall. Miss Dunn was directing Mrs Pettigrew as they arrived. The curate said, 'I'd like to have a word in private Miss Dunn, with yourself and Miss Proctor; maybe we could go into the choir vestry.' The two ladies followed him into the vestry and the door was firmly shut behind them. Everyone in the hall unashamedly strained their ears to hear what was said but nothing could be heard. When they finally emerged, Miss Dunn looked much the same as usual but Miss Proctor seemed to have grown a little in stature. From then on Miss Proctor was allowed full sway with the technical side of the musical items, although Miss Dunn still gave stage directions. Miss Dunn was as insensitive to comments made to her as she was to other people's feelings. No one would ever change Miss Dunn, one just had to learn how to live with her.

Mr Bulmer had persuaded the Acorn Morris Men to come along and perform. He was himself a member of the morris dance team, as was Mr Phillips. Unfortunately, the whole team could only attend the dress rehearsal and actual performance, so at Thursday rehearsals Mr Bulmer and Mr Phillips did a two-man version which necessitated a great deal of improvisation. Mr Bulmer was a large man and, as he and his partner galloped up and down the stage waving hankerchiefs, the floorboards bounced and the piano vibrated. The morris men would be bringing their own musicians along on the night but at rehearsals Miss Venables stood in for them and thumped Shepherd's Hey out on the piano.

The singing male trio comprised the Major, old Mr Bartholomew and Old Tom. They were to sing two numbers, one of which was 'Surrey with the Fringe on Top'. Miss Dunn had experienced difficulties in arranging the men on stage so that they looked aesthetically pleasing rather than ridiculous; it was a difficult task. The Major was tall, Mr Bartholomew was shorter with a slight stoop and Old Tom was short and wizened. Miss Dunn stood them in a line in descending order of height but they looked like three of the thirty-nine steps, so instead she put the Major in the middle. This didn't look right either; it was like planting a sunflower between a dahlia and a daisy. When sitting down they were similar heights but they then looked like the three wise monkeys – in any event they couldn't sing properly sitting down. Miss Dunn solved the problem in the end by arranging them in a crescent shape. Musically speaking, Miss Proctor was very pleased with them. They all had excellent voices and put heart and soul into their singing. Unfortunately this was their undoing one Thursday evening and they tried Miss Dunn's patience more than at any other time. She had already had a difference of opinion with all three of the maids from school and a heated discussion with Mr Turner on the lighting arrangements. 'Next item!' shouted Miss Dunn, '"Surrey with the Fringe on Top".'

The trio made their way on to the stage. Miss Proctor counted them in, one, two, three, four, and Miss Venables bounced along with them on the piano. 'I'm gonna take you out in the surrey,' boomed the Major, waving his arm in the air to emphasize the words. Old Tom opened his mouth and sang at the top of his voice, 'The dashboard's genuine leather.' Mr Bartholomew tapped one foot to the music and sang with great emphasis. Half-way through the refrain, however, Mr Bartholomew suddenly caught his breath and wheezed horribly. The Major was alarmed. 'Keep going!' shouted Miss Dunn, 'it's good practice, the show must go on.' Mr Bartholomew tried to keep singing but his lungs became uncooperative and he wheezed louder than ever and ended by coughing and wheezing alternately. The Major stopped singing and supported Mr Bartholomew by the arm. 'I say, steady old boy,' he said. Miss Dunn looked annoyed at the inconvenience of it all. Miss Venables' playing dwindled to a halt and Mrs Pettigrew went up on to the stage to see what she could do for Mr Bartholomew. The Major was suggesting a dose of whisky. 'I think not, Major,' said Mrs Pettigrew. 'I think Mr Bartholomew needs a quiet sit down and one of his tablets with a nice cup of tea, and then it's home to bed.' Mr Bartholomew sat down and the coughing stopped, but he still wheezed loudly. Miss Venables took her smelling salts from her handbag, but she was so upset by the sight of poor dear Mr Bartholomew that she had to use them herself. Mrs Pettigrew took Mr Bartholomew by the arm and led him through to the kitchen where she made him a cup of tea and said she would take him home in the car as soon as he had finished it.

'Can we please get on now?' called Miss Dunn. The Major and Old Tom came back on stage; 'Piano please,' said Miss Proctor but nothing happened. Miss Venables was still sniffing unhappily at her smelling salts. 'Piano!' roared Miss Dunn. Miss Venables was galvanized into action and off they went once more in the 'Surrey with the Fringe on Top'. Miss Dunn looked at her watch. They were behind schedule and it annoyed her. The Major and Old Tom sang louder than ever to make up for the lack of Mr Bartholomew, but the quality suffered. Old Tom became more enthusiastic as the song progressed. Opening his mouth wide he finished with an unrehearsed finale – suddenly his upper set of false teeth flew out of his mouth, hit the side of the stage and bounced off on to the floor. Miss Dunn looked with distaste at the dentures lying by her feet. Old Tom clambered off the stage and went to collect his property. Miss Dunn for once was lost for words; surely no director should have to put up with such impossible performers! Old Tom lovingly gathered up his dentures; they had broken in half and one incisor was chipped where it had caught the stage. The Major laughed till he cried and Miss Venables was suffused with hysterical mirth. Miss Dunn could not, herself, see anything remotely funny about the entire incident.

Miss Birch was bringing along a ladies' team of handbell ringers. It was something she participated in every other Tuesday evening. The handbell ringers were not from the church, but Miss Birch had persuaded them to come along and take part. Their exact performance remained a mystery. Like the morris men the only rehearsal they could attend was the dress rehearsal which, to Miss Dunn's dismay, was now only a couple of weeks away and there was still so much to be done.

THE DRESS REHEARSAL

The dress rehearsal commenced at seven o'clock. It went badly, which boded well for the actual performance. The vicar sent a note of apology to Miss Dunn to say that he had to take a confirmation class and was sorry he could not attend. 'Well, I hope everyone else doesn't have more important things to do, or there won't be a rehearsal,' retorted Miss Dunn. She had already been informed that the morris men would be arriving late.

The hall was in a state of undisguised chaos. Mr Turner had electric cables running across the entire width of the stage and at intervals called out 'Mind the wire,' even so, Miss Venables managed to trip over it and send sheet music in all directions. Mr Bulmer and Mr Newington were in their shirt sleeves and were engaged in shifting heavy scenery boards which had been left over from the Scout pantomine. Miss Dunn shouted instructions to move the piano further to the right and Mr Phillips and the Spotty Youth did their best to oblige. Mr Mitchell and the curate struggled to fix the curtains. Unfortunately these became stuck half-way across the stage and would neither fall back nor go forwards. Miss Dunn did not let this pass without comment, 'Audience isn't going to see much if it stays like that.' Mr Mitchell muttered something rather uncomplimentary under his breath, while the curate prayed for patience.

Miss Foggerty rushed round the hall with a box of pins and a needle and thread, making last minute adjustments. They discovered a moth-hole in Miss Peebles's kimono and hasty repairs were made. Miss Peebles pointed out that it must have already been in the vicarage curtains before they were made into the kimono, because she, personally, had no moths in *her* house. Lights flashed on and off as Mr Turner experimented with the lighting. Mr Mitchell and the curate were eventually successful in their attempt to fix the stage curtains; they suddenly flew back with a vengeance to reveal Mr Bulmer changing into his morris-dance outfit.

Mrs Pettigrew was to recite one of her poems and she was gargling and exercising her vocal cords. Miss Granger too was giving her vocals an airing and she warbled up and down the scale. Miss Peebles attempted to emulate her but the result was similar to a noisy hen laying an egg. Miss Proctor fussed over Jeremy's music stand, trying to adjust it to the correct height, while Miss Armitage warmed up on the cello. The curate stood centre-stage rehearsing his opening lines, 'Welcome to our Evening of Entertainment.' Miss Venables seated herself at the piano; she was wearing her long, black crêpe-de-Chine dress and she draped it effectively over the piano stool. Miss Peebles found a square yard of space at the far end of the hall and practised her dance steps. Holding out her left arm in what she considered to be a graceful pose, she arranged the right one around an imaginary Miss Granger and off she went, repeating to herself, 'Two to the right, left behind and – fiddle!' The kimono got caught on her shoe. Miss Dunn, clipboard in hand, climbed up on to the stage and shouted, 'Quiet everyone, rehearsals are going to begin now.'

The curate walked on to the stage and delivered his opening lines. After he had finished he announced the first item and walked off the stage into the wings. There was a crash followed by a muffled word which sounded like 'Blast', although it couldn't have been because the curate didn't use language like that. Jeremy's music stand was now a little bent in essential places.

After the Wives' Group, there followed an imaginary performance of 'Home Thoughts From Abroad' by the absent vicar and then it was time for Miss Venables to perform her piano piece. It was entitled 'The Tumbling Waterfall'. Miss Venables' piano playing was well-known in the parish but even so she excelled herself. Her fingers flew over the keys as the notes tumbled and fell like water over stones. She had placed a real rose in her hair and, towards the end of her faultless performance, the rose began to topple. As Miss Venables' piano playing involved her whole body, the movements caused the rose to slip over her left eye. Miss Venables, true artiste that she was, played on. She had reached the bar where the waterfall thundered into a canyon when the force behind the notes was too much for the rose. It detached itself completely and very neatly popped down inside the front of her dress. Miss Venables had, unfortunately, not removed all the thorns and she gave a screech of anguish as they scraped her skin. Miss Peebles rushed to her aid and they retired to the ladies' toilet to repair the damage. Miss Dunn tutted over this but before further comment could be made the curate stepped on stage and announced: 'Ladies and Gentlemen, please will you welcome Mrs

Pettigrew and her poem "Nightfall".' Mrs Pettigrew came forwards and tapped the curate gently on the arm and whispered something. The curate turned red and began apologizing, 'I'm so sorry, the poem is entitled, "Night-light", I mean "Twilight".' He brushed his sleeve across his perspiring forehead and exited quickly stage left. Crash went Jeremy's music stand, 'Blast' went the curate. Jeremy's music stand gained another dent and the curate acquired another bruise on the shin.

Mrs Pettigrew moved to the front of the stage and silence fell in the hall. Into the still air her soft, educated accents transported her listeners into the twilight. Mr Turner had an artistic turn with his lighting equipment. He dimmed the overhead lights and shone a blue light on Mrs Pettigrew. Her cerise evening dress turned a repulsive shade of mud, while her face became cyanosed and she looked terribly ill – for all the world like a grotesque spectre. 'Lights' commanded Miss Dunn, horrified. Mr Turner pressed a switch and all the lights went *off*. A gasp flew round the motley audience. With the aid of a hand torch Mr Turner illuminated the fault and made a very hasty repair. The lights flickered and then returned to normal. 'What are you trying to do, Mr Turner?' shouted a furious Miss Dunn. Mr Turner mumbled his apologies and muttered something about the moonlight and muted tones. Miss Dunn had no artistic leanings herself and had little patience with anyone who did. 'The audience want to be able to see Mrs Pettigrew, not be frightened out of their wits by a ghost. Please begin again Mrs Pettigrew.' Mr Turner muttered 'No sense of atmosphere' and busied himself with the fuse box. Half-way through 'Twilight' there was a disturbance at the back of the hall and Miss Birch's voice rang out saying, 'This way Mrs Fothergill,' and in trooped the team of handbell ringers. They unpacked their handbells, and assorted tinkles, clangs and bongs put an end to Mrs Pettigrew's cultured recitation.

The handbell ringers arranged themselves on the stage. Miss Birch played the two largest bells. Mrs Fothergill appeared to be in charge. She and Miss Dunn were like-spirits but they did not get on. Miss Dunn asked Mrs Fothergill to move nearer the front of the stage so that people could see better. Mrs Fothergill declined to move. She complained about the lighting, saying that it wasn't bright enough. A Mrs Glover took Miss Venables' place at the piano and wound the piano stool down as far as it would go. Miss Venables and Miss Proctor felt usurped, the piano stool was usually their domain and years ago it had been adjusted perfectly to suit them both and had never been touched since. Mrs Glover made a few derogatory remarks about the piano, asking if it had ever been tuned. Then Mrs Fothergill called her ladies to order and their rehearsal began. Never had anything like it been heard before in the church hall. The piano thumped out a rhythm while the bells clanged and crashed in cacophonous disharmony. *Ding dong, bong, clang, tinkle, tinkle* – 'Mrs Glover will you slow down a bit please . . . no, not that slow' – *clang, bang, dong, ding* – 'Mrs Pritchard! You missed it. Get ready for when it comes round again' – *ting, ding, clang, bong.* – 'Miss Peters, what do you think you are doing!' – *ding, clang, clong, bong.* 'Ladies, ladies, stop, stop, stop. It sounds dreadful. You're all out of sequence. Mrs Glover stop playing please . . . Mrs Glover shut up!' Silence. 'Now ladies, we are going to start again and this time will you please all concentrate. One, two, three and four . . . ' *Ding, dong, bong, clang – tinkle, ding, ding, bong.* – 'Oh, Mrs Pritchard! you missed it AGAIN' – *dinga, dinga, bong, clong, clang* – 'That's good ladies' – *clanga, clong, dong, bong, booma, bang, bong* – 'Miss Birch, not so loudly please, you're not ringing a ship's alarm bell you know' – *bong, clang, bong, clanga, bong, dong, dong* – 'Oh no! Mrs Pritchard, if you must drop your bell, please do it quietly next time' – *clong, clang, dong, bong, bong*!

Miss Venables was rather surprised to see 'nice Miss Pringle' from the haberdashers' ringing two of the handbells. She wondered how Miss Pringle fared amongst such hale and hearty bell ringing companions. Miss Birch donged her bells with gusto. Miss Dunn marched off to the kitchen for a cup of tea as a protest. When she eventually came back she found the bells still going; they were on their fourth number. 'I thought they were only down on the programme for two pieces,' said Miss Proctor to Miss Dunn. 'They are,' returned Miss Dunn. The two women looked at each other in unspoken agreement, for once united. It was now them against the enemy. 'Mrs Fothergill,' shouted Miss Dunn. She had to compete with a cacophony of discordant *dongs* and dissonant *dings* and it was difficult to make herself heard above the deafening clamour. Eventually Mrs Fothergill halted. Miss Dunn pointed out that the handbell ringers were only down on the programme for two pieces. 'But we always perform six pieces whenever we give a performance,' said Mrs Fothergill in a condescending manner. She considered herself a bit above Miss Dunn. Miss Dunn was only an old parish spinster, *she* was Mrs Fothergill, founder member of a very celebrated ladies' team of handbell ringers. For all the complaints about Miss Dunn, it could never be said that she gave herself airs and graces. She was always most down to earth and was now preparing to speak her mind. Fortunately Miss Birch intervened. 'Actually, think it would be better just to do the two, and perhaps a third one as an encore; only there are a lot of other acts to fit in.' 'Well, if you think so Miss Birch,' returned Mrs Fothergill in a gracious manner. 'I do,' said Miss Birch; 'the bishop's wife is coming and the bishop likes her home by half-past ten, so it can't go on too late.' How Miss Birch came by this riveting piece of information concerning the bishop's domestic arrangements no one knew, but it did have the effect of silencing Mrs Fothergill.

Next on stage was the singing male trio. Miss Dunn looked at them and despaired. She could have inserted the word 'geriatric' into their title. First the Major walked on with a walking stick and a canvas fishing stool. He explained, 'Leg's been giving me gyp.' He sat down on the fishing stool with his leg extended in front of him. Next was Mr Bartholomew, noisily sniffing at an inhaler. He politely informed Miss Dunn that he could only mime that evening; he was saving all his strength for the main performance. His doctor had told him to stay out of draughts and not to do anything strenuous. As a precaution against the draughts, Mr Bartholomew was wearing a furry Russian hat. Last on was Old Tom. Miss Dunn was momentarily relieved to see that Old Tom looked quite normal – that was until he opened his mouth. He was toothless. He gave Miss Dunn a most engaging gummy smile and explained that his top set was still being repaired, and that he couldn't wear the bottom set without the top ones because they chewed into his gums. The dentist had promised to get the teeth back for him by the day of the performance. Miss Venables spent ten minutes winding the piano stool back up and adjusting it to its old position. 'There won't be time for all that on the night,' commented Miss Dunn. Miss Venables replied that in that case Miss Dunn had better keep Mrs Glover's hands off it. Miss Venables played the intro. and 'Surrey with the Fringe on Top' got on the road. Well, really it got no further than the stable door, because only the Major was singing. Mr Bartholomew of course was miming, due to his infirmities, but what had happened to Old Tom? He was just standing there, looking all gums. The Major guessed why and started making gestures behind his ear. Old Tom laughed and turned on his hearing aid; he had previously turned it down as protection against the handbells. As he turned the hearing aid up it emitted a high pitched whistle. Miss Venables played the intro. again and off they rolled once more, along the country road in the 'Surrey with the Fringe on Top'. They went to the added accompaniment of a walking stick tapping the floor, wheezy inhalings, toothless singing and whistles from a hearing aid. Miss Dunn could have cried.

Next on stage were the three little maids. Hitching up their kimonos they navigated the steps and arranged themselves in a line. As they began to dance, Miss Peebles' kimono caught on her shoe and Mrs Mitchell, not knowing that Miss Peebles was going to stop suddenly, careered into her and their wigs fell off with the impact. Miss Granger kept on singing. 'Stop!' shouted Miss Dunn. Miss Foggerty made her way on to the stage and pinned up the hem of Miss Peebles' kimono and they began again. As they finished, the morris men arrived, wielding large sticks. They had bells on their legs which tinkled when they walked.

Miss Dunn was arranging Jeremy and Miss Armitage on stage. Miss Armitage looked most ungainly with her legs wrapped round the cello. Miss Dunn decided a sideways-on view would be better. Jeremy's music stand, after its unfortunate contretemps with the curate, was somewhat out of shape. Miss Proctor tried making adjustments to it, but the screw wouldn't turn properly and the top of the stand kept descending suddenly. Eventually, it was fixed to the best of Miss Proctor's ability and Miss Dunn gave the order to begin. Jeremy daintily lifted his flute to his mouth and Miss Armitage with bow poised over the strings gazed at Jeremy. Jeremy gave a slight inclination of his head and they began to play. Jeremy's fingers ran over the flute and a cascade of liquid notes fell from the instrument. Yet more notes soared into the air like soap bubbles; they hung, suspended for an instant, and then were gone. The cello began to harmonize with the flute as Miss Armitage gave herself up to the music and forgot about Jeremy. The harsh scraping of previous rehearsals gave way to a mellow harmonious sound. The clear full-bodied notes continued to filter through the flute and to fill the air with pure tones. The sweet sounds flowed like the balm of Gilead. Suddenly, with a violent crash, the music stand collapsed to the floor in a heap. Miss Armitage stopped in mid-scrape and Jeremy, who was of a sensitive nature, shrieked into the flute and jumped back as if shot. Miss Dunn suggested tying the music stand up with string. Miss Proctor said it wouldn't work. Mr Turner offered to take a hammer to it. Jeremy couldn't bear the thought of that and lovingly tried to fold the music stand up.

'Put the music on a chair and finish playing the piece,' ordered Miss Dunn. Jeremy looked, and felt, offended. How could he possibly play after what had just happened? He was still shaking from shock and his artistic temperament had been deeply affected. He could play no more tonight, he informed Miss Dunn. Miss Dunn couldn't care a fig about people's creative feelings and said so. Jeremy was so hurt, he was speechless. He took a clean white tissue from his music case and blew his nose, choking back the tears. It was all too much. He wasn't appreciated; he would never play for anyone ever again.

Mr Newington understood Jeremy's feelings and helped him off stage with his music case and the broken stand. Brandishing her bow in a threatening manner, Miss Armitage approached Miss Dunn saying, 'Now look what you've done.' 'I haven't done anything,' returned Miss Dunn, 'and I haven't got time to pander to people's tantrums. Now can we please get on?' Miss Armitage gave Miss Dunn a murderous look, which was entirely wasted as Miss Dunn was organizing the morris men. So she picked up her cello and joined Jeremy in the choir vestry. Jeremy had packed up his flute and put away his music. 'Jeremy dear,' began Miss Armitage, 'I think you were right not to play any more tonight.' 'Do you?' said Jeremy sadly, 'no one else thinks so.' Jeremy wrung his hands and tormented himself with feeling misunderstood. Miss Armitage sighed. Coping with Jeremy was not easy.

The morris men stomped up and down the stage waving handkerchiefs. It was mooted by the chief morris man, a Mr Turnbull, that the piano be moved off the stage on to the floor below to give them more room. As the piano had been on the stage since time immemorial, his suggestion met with general disapproval; the parishioners saw no reason to change the habit of a lifetime and, as no one wished to put their backs out by moving it, the piano stayed where it was. Miss Venables held her breath during one dance, as a pair of hefty morris men wielded large sticks at each other; one false move and she could see her ivories in fragments. As it was, she maintained that after the Entertainment the B flat was never quite the same again. She put it down to the vibration.

THE PERFORMANCE

It was Saturday teatime in the parish. The vicar finished his fourth cup of tea and held out his cup for a refill. 'Oh, to be in England now that April's here,' he recited. His wife was at screaming point, she could cheerfully have wrung Mr Browning's neck at that moment. For the last few days she hadn't been able to have a sensible conversation with him at all; Mr Browning had kept interrupting. Now her patience snapped. 'It isn't April; it's the end of October, and if you have any more to drink you know what will happen.' Sadly the vicar put his cup down; it wouldn't do to have to use the choir vestry toilet during the performance – the cistern had a remarkable repertoire of extremely loud wheezings and gurglings which could be heard from a great distance.

Mr Mitchell's family had just sat down to tea. Mr Mitchell decided that Miss Venables' knitted egg cosies had a lot to answer for as he fished woollen hairs out of his boiled egg and pondered on the forthcoming performance. Mr Turnbull, who was in charge of the morris dance team, had remarked that he hoped 'that Miss Dunn would keep her oar out'. So did Mr Mitchell, it wouldn't do to have any unpleasant scenes in front of the bishop's wife. He also sincerely hoped that young Jeremy had come to his senses.

Jeremy had bought his mother a new hat for the occasion. He fussed about arranging a feather in the brim. 'Now remember, Mother, you'll have to take it off for the performance or the people sitting behind you won't be able to see,' said Jeremy. 'Well, what's the sense in buying it, if I've got to take it off,' retorted his mother. 'You can wear it to church on Sundays,' he replied. Truth to tell, Jeremy himself had been enchanted by the hat and had bought it for that reason. After sorting his mother out, Jeremy swallowed two spoonfuls of valerian mixture to calm his nerves, drank a cup of camomile tea and went to have a lie down.

Miss Peebles lethargically toyed with a piece of toast and Marmite. Her stomach churned and did somersaults each time she thought of going on stage. She saw herself tripping over her kimono and making a spectacle of herself. Her cup of tea grew cold and the toast went soft. The hall clock chimed the hour and she jumped; she must hurry or she would be late. She looked at her untouched tea; it was no good, she couldn't swallow anything; she just hoped her stomach wouldn't object to the lost meal by rumbling during a quiet part of the performance.

Miss Venables told her three cats all about the evening's entertainment and explained that they must stay in for the evening because 'Mummy' was going out to play the piano. Miss Venables was highly excited by the occasion. This communicated itself to the cats who chased each other madly round the bedroom while Miss Venables put on her black crêpe-de-Chine.

Mr Newington secretly rehearsed his monologue 'just in case' then stood by the window to watch for Mr Turner who was to pick him up in the car.

Miss Birch had decided to entertain the entire ladies' team of handbell ringers by having them all to tea. Miss Birch was not one for dainty sandwiches. She had cut hunks of bread and cheese, thrown a few tomatoes and some lettuce leaves into a bowl and buttered a dozen currant buns. No one complained, they were a hale and hearty bunch, that is with the exception of 'nice Miss Pringle' who sat nervously in one corner, munching a piece of Cheddar like a timid mouse. Miss Birch and Mrs Fothergill barked at each other over the buns.

The curate's housekeeper ironed his cassock for the occasion and put out a newly starched, crisp, clean, dog collar.

Mr Bulmer set out rows of chairs in the hall. In the front row an armchair had been placed for the bishop's wife to sit in. At a quarter-past seven the audience began to arrive. Miss Willis entered, majestically, wearing a fur stole that looked as if it had done battle in the Crimea. She deposited herself next to Miss Whitticks, who had tucked all her animals up and come out for a night on the tiles. She had brought along one cousin who smelt of dogs and another who smelt of horses. Later in the evening she introduced Miss Willis to her brother who was a farmer. Miss Willis did not care to think what *he* smelt of.

There was a rustling of programmes and murmured conversation, as the audience anticipated the forth-coming performance. The vicar's wife hung about outside the church waiting for the arrival of the bishop's wife. The vicar had just been made up by Miss Foggerty and now joined his wife by the railings, muttering 'Oh, to be in England'. The morris men had a disagreement with Miss Dunn, who told them to 'Remove those wretched bells from your legs; they make so much noise the audience won't be able to hear the other performers.' Before Mr Turnbull could reply, Miss Dunn was saying, 'Miss Granger, don't forget to wave as you go off the stage; you did last time.' Miss Granger opened her mouth to say she wouldn't forget, but Miss Dunn was dashing up on to the stage to remind Mr Turner not to try anything fancy with the lights.

The choir vestry which had now been turned into a dressing-room was not large enough for all the performers to change at once. It was decided that those who were appearing in the second half should sit in the audience and enjoy the first part of the show. They would change during the interval.

The three little maids were due on at the beginning of the second half, so they sat in the audience as requested. Miss Peebles felt sick. Why had she ever agreed to this? Nervously she loosened the collar of her dress. Jeremy was 'resting' upstairs in the church. Mr Newington was to call him down at the appropriate time. Miss Dunn fussed over the position of the piano, checked that Old Tom had his teeth in and reminded the curate to look where he was going when he walked into the wings. Mr Bartholomew appeared much recovered and he and the Major looked most dashing in their dinner jackets.

The Miss Jameses arrived with Jeremy's mother and sat down behind Miss Willis. Miss Venables's brothers arrived with their families. Roger and

Stephen kept asking in loud voices where Auntie was. They discussed in vivid detail what would happen if the piano lid suddenly fell down while Auntie Letti was playing. They disagreed as to whether her fingers could be sewn back on. Miss Peebles, on overhearing this, suddenly felt in need of a breath of fresh air and slipped outside.

Miss Dunn adjusted the large bow in Miss Armitage's hair, shouted at Mr Mitchell to check that the stage curtains were working and peered through a crack in the door to see if the bishop's wife had arrived. The hall was packed to capacity. Mr Rushmore counted the one-and-sixpences and was well pleased with the amount. Mrs Turner and Mrs Newington took their seats and craned their necks to see who had turned up for the event.

Miss Dunn was in a high state of agitation; she had lost the vicar. She hurried to the kitchen to see if he was there, as it was well-known that the vicar and a teapot were inseparable companions. Unbeknown to her, the vicar had felt – and looked – somewhat ridiculous standing outside wearing a thick layer of face powder and eye-liner and his wife had suggested he go back inside. The vicar returned to the hall by way of a side door, just missing Miss Dunn as she tore along to the kitchen.

Mrs Fothergill gave last minute instructions to her handbell ladies, while Miss Venables rifled through a music case. There was a moment of panic when it appeared that she had left 'The Tumbling Waterfall' at home, but it was found caught up in 'Count Your Blessings' which the male trio were doing for an encore, that is, if they got one.

There was an awed murmur as the bishop's wife arrived. Escorted by Mr Rushmore and the vicar's wife, she made her way to the front row. The Entertainment could now start. After Miss Venables had played 'God Save the Queen' and everyone had resumed their seats, the curate appeared on stage. He welcomed the audience and announced the singing wives. The curtains were pulled back; for a dreadful moment it seemed that they would stick, but Mr Mitchell gave a hefty pull and they flew back.

Meanwhile, Miss Dunn was searching in the church for the vicar, but the only person she found was Jeremy 'resting' on a pew, and doing deep-breathing exercises. Eventually she gave up and made her way back to the hall. As she arrived in the vestry she heard with relief the vicar's voice coming from the stage saying, 'Oh, to be in England'. The performance was well and truly under way.

The Epidemic

It was Saturday afternoon and the church was full of strangers. They were milling around and conversing in subdued tones. This year our church was hosting a performance of Handel's Messiah and parishioners from neighbouring churches were joining forces with us to sing this great oratorio. Our resident church choir let their superiority be known by discussing the music at such a great intellectual depth that even Handel would have been confused. Saturday afternoon was the rehearsal. Those of us not in the church choir waited impatiently for the conductor to stop drinking tea and get on with it.

The church was damp and cold and I was not feeling my best. My throat was dry and dusty and I had a horrible suspicion that it was the start of something nasty. The conductor, Mr Alexander Forbes, had spent a considerable time arranging us. Several front rows of pews had been turned round to face the audience and chairs had been placed in the chancel. The afternoon dragged interminably, with the church growing colder by the minute, or so it seemed to me. At teatime I could not do justice to any of Miss Dunn's great spread of food. I would rather have gone home. At six-thirty the audience arrived and I wished they could all have gone home too. For the performance, the ladies had to wear long black skirts and white blouses. I had a jumper on under mine. Miss Armitage adjusted the bow in my hair and I fastened a gold cross round her neck. We filed into the church. The organ joined a selection of wind and stringed instruments to play the overture.

Everyone in the enlarged choir had a paperback edition of the Messiah, except me. I had decided to use an antique score which had been handed down to me. It was a hardback edition with gilt-edged pages and weighed a ton. My sense of the historical outweighed my common sense. I forgot that I would have to hold it up in front of me for some several hours. Mr Forbes waved his baton upwards which meant 'Get up all you lot in the chorus'. So we stood and sang, *'And the glory, the glory of the Lord shall be revealed,'* (I don't 'alf feel cold) *'Shall be revealed. For the mouth of the Lord has spoken it'*, which was more than mine could as my voice was going. Like two pieces of coarse sandpaper the sides of my throat rasped and scratched. We had no sooner sat down, than we were up again: *'Oh thou that tellest good tidings to Zion'* (I feel sick) *'Arise, arise'* (I want to sit down) *'Say unto the cities'* (I think I've got flu). We reached the end of the chorus and I sank into the chair feeling miserable.

A visiting professional singer with a bass voice rose, and holding his stomach sang, *'For behold darkness shall cover the earth.'* This was much more in keeping with how I felt. Then it was time to sing again. *'For unto us a child is born'* (This book's so heavy) *'Unto us a Son is given'* (My arms ache) *'and the government shall be upon his shoul . . .'* (Mustn't drop this book) *'. . .der, and his name shall be called'* (I must remain upright) *'Wonderful'*. I subsided on to the hard chair while the Pastoral Symphony gave me a welcome respite.

Mrs Brampton-Jones then arose. She wore a creation in vivid mauve set about with sequins, over which she wore a massive cape lined with fur. I shivered in my thin blouse. Mrs Brampton-Jones could have kept warm with her fat alone, never mind all the trappings. I could have used her cape. These unMessiah-like thoughts kept me occupied while she warbled through her recitative. Then we had to stand and sing *'Glory to God in the highest'*. My voice cracked and packed up. I mimed the rest and concentrated on how to act looking well. We moved with unerring slowness through Part the Second. *'All we like sheep have gone astray . . .'* (I feel dreadful) *'We have tu-ur-urned'* (Got to keep standing) *'Everyone to his own way'*. The Hallelujah Chorus passed in a mist of nauseous shivers. We were then into Part the Third. Mr Forbes flourished and waved his baton mouthing silent instructions. I mouthed back the words of the Messiah and we performed a duet of mime. Finally the Amen Chorus was upon us. *'Amen, Amen'*. Anna whispered the old adage about it being the answer to a maiden's prayer. *'Ah, ah, ah, ah Amen'* (A-a-a-a-ahtishoo) *'Amen, amen, amen'*. Then Amen! It was time to go home.

When I arrived home my mother discovered I had a temperature of one-hundred-and-three and I crawled into bed, there to dream of copies of the Messiah which got bigger and BIGGER and BIGGER until I woke screaming. Influenza took over the next few days. Eventually I was able to take in the snippets of parish gossip that were brought to me. The parishioners were being struck down like Sodom and Gomorrah as the flu epidemic rampaged through the parish. Just imagine the parishioners trying to cope with events. . .

The vicar announced at January's PCC meeting that he would be going into hospital to have an ingrowing toe-nail removed and also that he had made arrangements for the curate to have some ecclesiastical help. The first statement had an effect on Mr Newington, who hurried home after the meeting and lost no time in making an in-depth study of his toe-nails with the aid of a dental mirror. The second statement had an effect on the whole parish, not least on Mr Crumpton. The vicar had arranged that the Reverend Poddlewell's curate would help out on Sundays. Mr Crumpton nearly resigned. He knew instinctively that any curate of the Reverend Poddlewell's would have gone to a charismatic theological college and passed out the other end full of love, joy and Jesus stickers.

Miss Dunn voiced an opinion loud and clear when she received the news. 'You know what that will mean,' she said to anyone who was listening, 'it means guitars in the nave,' and with that she pursed her lips and went off to make her feelings on the subject known to the vicar.

At the beginning of February, the vicar retired to the local cottage hospital leaving Mr Crumpton in charge. Mr Crumpton lost no time in instigating a few minor adjustments to the forthcoming Sunday service. He considered the wisdom of having a few wafts of incense, but decided that, much as he enjoyed it himself, others might not share his predilection. Instead, he persuaded the choir master to teach the choirboys to sing something in Latin.

It was a Saturday morning and Mr Crumpton was just toying with the idea of a few extra candles on the altar when the side door banged and an apparition in faded jeans appeared, wearing a floppy T-shirt with 'LOVE' emblazoned across the front. 'Hi,' said the apparition. 'Oh,' said the curate. 'Happiness and peace be with you Brother,' continued the apparition. 'Yes, well . . .,' responded Mr Crumpton, dusting his hands down his cassock and moving sideways like a crab towards the vestry. Blue Jeans bounded up the chancel steps and extended a hand towards Mr Crumpton. 'Albert, I believe,' he said. Mr Crumpton's stomach sank to his boots, he had just had the most 'orrible thought. It was soon confirmed by Blue Jeans, who said 'My name's Dave, I'm curate to Sydney Poddlewell.' Mr Crumpton, ignoring the outstretched hand, said resignedly, 'I think you'd better come into the vestry then.'

As the two men disappeared into the vestry, Miss Dunn came in through the main door and began banging about at the back of the church. She was using the hymn-book table to lay out piles of parish magazines. Miss Dunn was in charge of parish magazines. This meant that she didn't deliver them but organized the good souls who did. Each batch of magazines had the person's name written on a piece of scrap paper clipped to the top. The paperclips used in this procedure always had to be returned by placing them in a special receptacle, in this case an empty cottage-cheese tub. Failure to do so resulted in severe reprimand. Many of these slips of paper bore messages: 'Miss Foggerty; don't forget to deliver at No. 19.' 'Miss Peebles; No.5 Willow Tree Avenue owes 6d – make her pay up.' 'Miss Whitticks; keep these away from Rover.' 'Miss Venables; if you shove these through the wrong doors again there won't be any replacements.'

Miss Dunn had just finished sorting the magazines and was about to investigate a dead flower arrangement when the vestry door opened and out came a flustered, red-faced Mr Crumpton, followed by a 'Hippy'. The hippy said 'Farewell, Brother, see you next week,' and left through the side door. Miss Dunn was most interested. Mr Crumpton sat down on a pew and took out a large handkerchief and mopped his brow with it. Miss Dunn grabbed a parish magazine and hurried over to the curate.

Proffering the magazine she said, 'Here's this month's *Parish News* – er – did the young gentleman come to ask when the services were, or maybe he wants to get married?' Miss Dunn stood expectantly over Mr Crumpton, waiting for an answer. The curate seemed to have difficulty in answering that question; finally he blurted out, 'No, he's not getting married; he'll be doing the marrying.' Miss Dunn looked puzzled. The curate clarified his statement. 'The young gentleman is my ecclesiastical help, courtesy of the Revered Poddlewell.' 'You don't mean he's a curate?' exploded Miss Dunn. Mr Crumpton nodded miserably. His head ached, his throat hurt and he felt hot and cold all over. On top of which he'd been sent a thorn in the flesh in the form of Brother Blue Jeans, and now Miss Dunn was hovering over him like the Sword of Damocles. The load was too much even for a curate.

Miss Dunn lost no time in spreading the tidings round the parish. By the time Miss Peebles received the news late on Saturday afternoon, the locum curate was a flower-power, pot-smoking, free-loving Hippy, who was going to do away with services altogether and hold group therapy meetings in the church garden, where they could all have a free psychedelic experience. Miss Venables was quite thrilled at the idea. Miss Peebles told her to calm down because she was sure the bishop wouldn't allow any 'goings on'. 'I wonder if he's got a guitar?' said Miss Venables dreamily; yes, she really was longing to meet the new curate. She would have to wait until the following Sunday when he commenced his duties. Meanwhile Mr Crumpton comforted himself with the fact that at least he would have *this* Sunday to himself; but it was not to be.

On Sunday morning as he ascended the pulpit steps they seemed to him to be made of jelly; they wobbled and swayed. His head still ached; he thought it must be the worry of Blue Jeans. When he looked out at his congregation they seemed far away and, before long, they too, swayed and wobbled like the steps. Mr Crumpton began to preach. His throat felt like a nutmeg-grater and his nose appeared to be full of a thousand tickling feathers. Half-way through the sermon he sneezed heartily, the draught of which sent his sermon notes fluttering down over the pulpit to bury themselves in an arrangement of evergreens. Mr Crumpton hastily ended his sermon by saying the grace, and shakily made his way back down the steps. After the service he 'came over funny' in the vestry and the churchwardens made arrangements for him to be taken home in a car. They promised to find someone to wheel his beloved bicycle home for him. Mr Newington hurried home so that he could disinfect his nasal passages. He understood germs could be airborne and he had been in direct line of the curate's sneeze.

It was obvious that the evening service would have to be cancelled. Miss Proctor was asked to pin a notice to the church door to this effect. After much pencil chewing Miss Proctor came up with what she considered a Very Official Notice. It took a while to get to the point and read as follows: 'Due to unforseen circumstances and the said circumstances beyond our immediate control, we regrettably have to announce to parishioners and any visitors visiting our parish that due to unexpected illness we have had to cancel our evening service. We apologize for any inconvenience caused, but wish to point out that the PCC are not liable for any claims, made by any persons, for any damages which may arise as a result of the cancellation of this meeting. This includes any loss, destruction or damage due to any fire, explosion, lightning, Act of God, thunderbolt, riots, subterranean fire, earthquake, storm, flood, tempest or civil-commotion resulting from the cancellation of the above meeting. Normal service will be resumed as soon as possible.' That, she felt, covered everything.

When Miss Peebles arrived for the evening service she found that someone had scribbled at the bottom of the notice in red ink 'No evening service', which was much more to the point. The church door was not locked and Miss Peebles opened it and went inside to collect her batch of magazines. Miss Dunn had made some rearrangements. Attached to Miss Peebles' pile of magazines was yet another note which read 'Please deliver Miss Foggerty's magazines, Miss F. in bed with flu.' Miss Peebles sighed and picked up the two bundles, she then searched for the pile with Miss Venables' name on them. Her friend had been unable to swallow her Sunday crumpet at teatime and Miss Peebles feared that she would be the next one to succumb to the flu virus. Miss Peebles was about to leave the church when Miss Dunn burst forth from the vestry and panted up the nave. 'Miss Peebles,' called Miss Dunn in a loud stage whisper. Miss Peebles halted by the poor box and waited for Miss Dunn to catch up. Miss Dunn snatched a pile of magazines off the table and thrust them at Miss Peebles. 'Please would you be so good as to deliver these? Miss James has got a high temperature and her sister's not feeling too good so they won't be well enough to take these round.' Miss Peebles muttered something about the ten little niggers and accepted the large bundle of magazines. Looking at the amount she had to deliver, she thought it unlikely that she would have finished by the time next month's edition came out.

The following week saw Miss Peebles tramping the streets of the parish each afternoon delivering magazines and collecting outstanding subscriptions. One afternoon she bumped into Mr Newington who was on a similar mission. A glum Mr Newington informed her that his wife was now in bed with the virus. Mr Newington had not been having a very good week. At the first sign of his wife's illness, he had moved his pyjamas and pillow into the spare bedroom, sterilized all the crockery and utensils used by his wife and kept his distance. He and Miss Peebles discussed the epidemic. Miss Peebles told him how swollen Miss Venables' tonsils were. Mr Newington swallowed nervously, he could feel something . . . he knew it, the flu had struck! He bade a hurried goodbye to Miss Peebles and without finishing his magazine round he hurried home to inspect his tonsils. He was not quite certain what they looked like but was sure he would know one when he saw it. Meanwhile, Miss Peebles trudged up Willow Tree Avenue.

The following Sunday saw the arrival of Mr Poddlewell's curate. Miss Venables sat up in bed and bemoaned to her cats that she would miss all the fun. Dave arrived in the vestry half an hour before the start of Holy Communion. Dressed in his usual faded blue jeans and a T-shirt which today shouted the message 'PEACE' he proceeded to pull his Holy Vestments on over the top, much to Mr Bulmer's disgust. Somehow it didn't seem quite right. Mr Crumpton always wore clerical black under *his* vestments. Snapping his fingers and singing 'Oh Happy Day' the new curate jigged over to inspect the sacraments. Mr Bulmer, knowing that the vicar normally liked a few quiet moments to himself before the service, inconspicuously left the vestry. Upon his return ten minutes later he found the curate with one leg up on a pile of prayer-books strumming a guitar and singing, 'He's got the whole world in His hands'. Mr Bulmer hurried straight out again.

It would be best not to recall the events of the service, suffice to say that afterwards the congregation became divided into two camps – pro and anti the curate. The fact that he wore denims under his vestments soon became public knowledge; Miss Willis thought it scandalous and wrote to the bishop. After the service, the diminished congregation loitered outside to exchange their weekly news. Miss Whitticks told Miss Birch and Mr Newington that she had had to take Rover to the vet for his inoculations against hard pad. Mr Newington had hard skin under his left foot and he began to wonder if humans could get hard pad. However, before he had time to wonder too much, Miss Dunn came over bursting with importance – as always the bearer of news. 'Have you heard about Mr Bartholomew?' she asked with relish. All within hearing shook their heads. Pleased with this reaction, Miss Dunn became all confidential and spoke in a voice of impending doom and disaster. Miss Proctor had in fact been the first to hear about Mr Bartholomew from his next-door neighbour when she had delivered his parish magazine. The truth of the matter was that old Mr Bartholomew was recovering from a bad bout of bronchitis and his GP had decided that, owing to the virulent nature of the flu epidemic, his wheezy patient would be safer in the isolation wing of the hospital, where he would be relatively free from germs and where he could be cared for should any complications arise. Therefore, one sunny afternoon Mr Bartholomew, well muffled against the wind, packed himself and a supply of books into the Major's car and betook himself to the cottage hospital. However, this was not how it was reported along the congregational grapevine. By the time the news reached Miss Dunn it had been well-embroidered and embellished and Miss Dunn now proposed to do it justice in front of her audience. According to Miss Dunn it happened like this: Mr Bartholomew had been rushed to hospital by ambulance at three o'clock in the morning, choking to death. The flu virus had invaded his lungs and he had stopped breathing. Mr Newington suddenly felt a constriction across his chest. He knew he couldn't escape the flu much longer. He was also worried because he had lost his tonsils.

In the general upheaval, everyone had forgotten that the bishop was paying a visit to the parish on the following Sunday. Mr Bulmer, whose mind had been occupied with keeping the locum curate under control, had a shock when he made the discovery in his diary on the Friday morning. He hurried at once to call upon Mr Crumpton, whose housekeeper, a rather sour woman in a faded overall, admitted Mr Bulmer with a disdainful sniff and disappeared to the back of the house, from whence issued a pungent odour of boiled cabbage.

Mr Bulmer entered the curate's study. Mr Crumpton was seated in a dilapidated armchair by a small coal fire which was smoking in the grate. Mr Crumpton was convalescing. He still wore his clerical black with his white dog collar, over which he wore a moth-eaten grey cardigan. Peeping beneath his black robe were a pair of worn tartan carpet slippers. The curate's big toe stuck out through a hole in the left slipper. The wallpaper in the study had faded to shades of brown and the whole gloomy picture was completed by the dismal brown linoleum on the floor. A smelly rag rug of hideous purple shouted its existence from in front of the fire. The curate had his feet on the fender and a copy of the *Church Times* on his lap. Viewing the depressing scene, Mr Bulmer felt it was time the synod reviewed the curate's stipend. The flu had left Mr Crumpton with a chesty cough and not much voice; he gesticulated to a chair on the other side of the fire. Before he could sit down, Mr Bulmer had to remove a quantity of past editions of the *Church Times*, a leaflet on the breeding habits of the death-watch beetle and a half-eaten cheese sandwich, the mould on which would have excited Alexander Fleming.

Mr Crumpton was most agitated when he learnt of the bishop's impending visit, and he proceeded to croak a list of instructions to Mr Bulmer. Mr Bulmer promised to make the necessary preparations and to arrange transport on Sunday to and from the church for Mr Crumpton who insisted that it was his bounden duty to be there. Mr Bulmer did point out that Mr Poddlewell's curate would be in attendance, but poor Mr Crumpton was so distressed by this thought that it brought on one of his coughing fits. Mr Bulmer stood up to take his leave, stepping as he did so on a garibaldi biscuit which was half hidden under a copy of St John's Gospel. After Mr Bulmer had departed, the curate felt at an all-time low. This was not helped by the sight of his housekeeper who had arrived to announce that 'Yer dinner's ready', and the unappetizing odour of boiled cabbage and cod (the curate was rather RC about Fridays) did nothing to lift his drooping spirits.

Miss Peebles had received a message from Miss Dunn asking if she would help clean the church on Saturday morning. Sunday school superintendents did not normally dust pews but Miss Peebles realizing it was an emergency had agreed to help. When she arrived at ten o'clock the church was already a hive of industry. The normal segregation of appointed duties had gone by the board this time, owing to the fact that more than half the congregation were laid up with the flu, and it was a question of 'all shoulders to the wheel'. Upon arrival, Miss Peebles was handed a cobweb brush and asked to remove the cobwebs that were hanging off the pillars. Miss Birch suggested that Miss Peebles also ought to stick it behind the radiators because 'That's where the spiders hang out.' Miss Peebles had no intention of doing so. Apart from the fact that she had no wish to evict a large, angry spider, she very much doubted that the bishop would have time to peer behind the radiators on Sunday anyway.

Miss Dunn sorted out the altar linen while Mr Newington ran the vacuum cleaner over the nave carpet. Jeremy was squatting by the altar rail dexterously re-covering a hassock in red velvet. This substantial hassock which only saw the light of day on important occasions had, unfortunately, been ravaged by mice during the winter. Every so often thunderous rumblings emanated from the organ pipes as Miss Proctor practised a processional march. Miss Birch polished the brasses while Miss Armitage whisked a duster over the pews. Miss Dunn didn't like it, it was most unorganized. It became more so as the morning went on.

Miss Willis was attempting an artistic creation of white lilies and assorted ferns at the bottom of the chancel steps when she stepped back to view her arrangement and knocked over a large enamel jug full of water. The tide of water spread rapidly across the floor *en route* for the nave carpet. Miss Birch had been enthusiastically polishing the eagle on the lectern when the accident happened and, from her vantage point on the lectern, she could see that the nave carpet was in grave danger. Without more ado, she leant forward on the eagle and attempted to fling her polishing rag on top of the spreading puddle. To her dismay the head suddenly dropped off the eagle. Hilary Birch, who was no light weight, was left open-mouthed, clinging to its brass body, whilst everyone gasped at this new momentous catastrophe. It was not entirely Miss Birch's fault. The poor bird had an unfortunate history. Many years before, the roof rafters had undergone restoration and a cross beam had somehow been dislodged during the work. It had crashed to the ground, destroying the lectern and the first few rows of pews. Fortunately no one had been hurt but the lectern had been completely shattered. Under the debris they found the eagle in two parts, its head having been guillotined in the accident. By the time a new lectern had been provided there was no money left to purchase a new eagle so the old one had been repaired. The welding had provided a weak point. No one quite knew what to say, except Mr Bulmer who stared at it in shock-horror and said, 'The bishop!' He and Mr Mitchell hurried away for a quick conference on how you made instant repairs to brass eagles.

While everyone had been transfixed by the eagle's sudden demise, the spilt water had insidiously crept unnoticed into the nave carpet, and a dark blue patch was now becoming evident. Cloths, mops and dusters were quickly put to work on the damp patch but the thick, felt-like carpet soaked the water up like a sponge and, short of taking it up and trying to wring it out, there was nothing to be done except wait for the natural drying-out process. Mr Newington had by now progressed with his vacuum cleaner to the chancel. Miss Dunn had just said, 'I hope nothing else goes wrong,' when the bag on the vacuum cleaner burst and an explosion of dust billowed into the air and fell like nuclear fall-out on to the newly dusted choir stalls. By lunch-time the parishioners had not really made much progress and they all agreed they would have to return in the afternoon. Miss Birch, in an attempt to make amends for her unfortunate accident, volunteered to bring her vacuum cleaner from home.

She returned in the afternoon with the vacuum cleaner strapped to her moped. Inside the church, Jeremy was holding the eagle's head while Mr Turner, who had been dragged from his sick bed, attempted to reunite head and body with a soldering iron. Progress was slow. Mr Newington had asked Miss Armitage if she could help him find his tonsils and when Miss Dunn returned from lunch she found Mr Newington standing with his mouth open under a stained-glass window while Miss Armitage, who was perched on a pew, attempted to position him so that the coloured light from the window illumined his throat. Miss Dunn for once was speechless. It confirmed her belief that she was the only sane individual in the whole parish.

At four o'clock the choir boys arrived for a practice. The choirmaster was ill and his place was taken by

Dave, Mr Poddlewell's curate. The eagle had been mended to the best of everyone's ability and Mr Turner had gone back to bed. The brass eagle now sported a thick lumpy collar of silver solder and its head veered slightly to the left. With the bishop's visit imminent it was decided to assist the drying process of the wet carpet by placing two stone hot-water bottles on it overnight. These were kindly lent by Miss Willis. She had now completed her flower arrangement but due to the general hiatus she had forgotten to fill the vase with water. As the night passed, so the flowers drooped . . .

Early on Sunday morning Mr Bulmer unlocked the church. Jeremy had agreed to stand in for Mr Turner and he too arrived early. They met in the vestry and were soon joined by Mr Newington. Mr Newington was, this morning, having trouble with a tickle in his throat and a blocked nose. Mr Bulmer said it was probably brought on by all the dust from the vacuum cleaner. Jeremy said he was a great believer in garlic capsules for keeping germs away. Mr Newington, ever interested in new pills and potions, asked for more details. Jeremy dug into his overcoat pocket and pulled out a small pill-bottle. He tipped several pills out and handed them to Mr Newington. Eagerly Mr Newington popped them in his mouth and chewed. Jeremy looked aghast; Mr Newington began to turn purple in the face. 'You're supposed to swallow them whole with water, and then only two capsules twice daily!' said an incredulous Jeremy. Mr Newington spluttered and rolled his eyes. Mr Bulmer thumped him on the back. An overpowering smell of garlic began to fill the vestry. Mr Newington finally swallowed the remains of the capsules and hastily reached for a slug of communion wine, this being the only liquid to hand. A few seconds later he developed a bad attack of the hiccups. Reverend Blue Jeans chose this moment to arrive, today flamboyant in a scarlet T-shirt with 'I'm H.A.P.P.Y.' stamped on it. Mr Bulmer thought it a good job somebody was. 'Gosh,' said Dave, 'smells like a French restaurant in here.'

Miss Venables had refused to be dissuaded from attending Holy Communion that morning. Miss Peebles had said it really wasn't worth getting pneumonia just to see the bishop. However, it was not the bishop that Miss Venables wished to see; it was the new curate. She had heard delightful things about him from Miss Proctor who was quite smitten. Besides, Miss Proctor had also mentioned that she was playing something rather fun on the organ and Miss Venables was intrigued.

Timid Miss Proctor had, surprisingly, hit it off with the charismatic curate at their first meeting. Dave did not have the awsome personality of the other Reverend Gentlemen she had previously encountered. He had a warm gentle disposition and a great sense of humour. The floppy sloganed T-shirts he wore helped her to forget that he was a curate. She even found herself sharing her secret about the little brown mouse who lived in the vestry. Dave shared Miss Proctor's love of music and in preparation for the bishop's visit they had had a wonderful musical evening together. Miss Proctor had lost herself in a forest of tinkling notes on the piano while the curate had strummed himself into a trance on his guitar.

Mr Crumpton arrived at the church in the Major's car. He still felt very shaky but was most anxious that 'Me Lord Bishop' would find a smoothly run parish. He was in for a disappointment. When he arrived in the vestry he was greeted by a loud hiccup from Mr Newington and nearly bowled over by garlic fumes. A half-consumed bottle of communion wine stood on the vicar's desk. Mr Bulmer was busily handing round peppermints and Reverend Blue Jeans was precariously seated on a pile of hymn-books in the corner, strumming his guitar and singing 'Give me oil in my lamp, keep me burning'. Mr Crumpton very uncharitably wished his lamp would go out, and preferably stay out. Miss Proctor rushed in at that moment and pressed some milk of magnesia tablets into Mr Newington's hand and rushed out again, giving Blue Jeans a flashing smile and a thumbs up sign on the way. The vestry door opened again and Miss Willis hurried through with a water jug, saying that the flowers were all dead. The curate felt his head spinning. Jeremy knocked on the door and announced that the bishop's car had just arrived. Mr Bulmer and Jeremy hurried out to greet him, while Mr Crumpton attempted to follow them, coughing all the way.

Bishop Horatio stepped out of his car wearing his full vestments and carrying a brown suitcase containing his mitre. He was a stately man of large proportions. Mr Bulmer shook him warmly by the hand while helpful Jeremy slammed the car door. It was only when the bishop went to walk away that he found he couldn't; Jeremy had trapped his alb in the car door. This was a very inauspicious start. If the bishop was surprised at the unusual odour in the vestry, he was too polite to say anything. The clergy and the choir got ready to process round the church. This was ostensibly so that everyone could have a good view of the bishop but really because Mr Crumpton loved a nice procession. Jeremy was to stand in as an acolyte and Miss Armitage ensconced herself in a front pew so as not to miss anything.

The church, which was normally full, looked sadly depleted in numbers that morning. Whole pews remained empty and the congregation was dotted about in twos and threes. The sidesmen had endeavoured to make everyone sit in the main pews and not spread out to the side aisles. They did not have much success. People wanted to sit where they always sat every Sunday and they did not intend to move even for a bishop. The clergy were ready. The organ wheezed as Miss Proctor coaxed it into life. She pulled out all the stops and pressed her foot down on the loud pedal. Miss Proctor was nervous. Her fingers slipped as she played the first chord of the processional march and the church was filled with a vibrating dissonance which sounded very much as if the roof was caving in. Mr Crumpton muttered apologies to the bishop. Miss Proctor made a second attempt and the procession commenced. As they turned from the side aisle to process down the nave, the bishop caught sight of what appeared to be two large boulders in the middle of the carpet. Mr Crumpton swallowed hard as two of his congregation leapt from their pews and gathered up the stone hot-water bottles, which had been left in place until the last moment and had then been forgotten.

The bishop, looking dignified and stately with mitre and crook, brought up the rear of the procession. Miss Willis gave him a withering glance as he passed her. The bishop had not answered her letter with regard to Reverend Blue Jeans and she was a little miffed to say the least. The procession slowed down as the choir made their way up the chancel steps into the choir stalls. Mr Crumpton feared that his temperature had gone up again, as it felt to him as if the carpet was squelching under his feet. As the bishop passed one pew he noticed a stone hot-water bottle sitting on top of a hassock. He knew that churches were notoriously cold but surely warming a kneeler before one used it was taking things a little too far. The bishop had now reached the end of the nave and with surprise he felt his feet come into contact with a soggy carpet. He continued with dignity past the dead lilies and made his way up through the choir stalls. With a sigh of relief he made to lower himself into the bishop's chair, which had been specially polished by Miss Birch for the occasion. It had in fact, been excessively polished and the bishop's reverential posterior skidded across the highly glossed wooden seat. He clutched the chair arms to steady himself, but these had been burnished by Miss Birch to an even finer degree than the seat and his hands nimbly skated off the supports. As he hurtled forwards he grabbed a carved Cherubim by the foot and successfully heaved himself into reverse. Eventually seated in an upright position he momentarily solved the problem by wedging his black clerical boots behind the substantial hassock. With his customary reverence, Mr Crumpton seated himself. In the compartment before him, where he expected to take hold of a well-thumbed copy of the Ancient and Modern, he instead found himself holding an ancient pair of Mr Twig's underpants, courtesy of the cleaning corps.

Miss Armitage had not taken her eyes off Jeremy as he had glided solemnly past bearing his candle. Miss Proctor concluded the processional march with a final chord on the organ and there followed a silence while the congregation seated themselves. Mr Crumpton was on the point of speaking when Jeremy, who had just placed his candle in its holder, suddenly gave a violent sneeze. The candle and two others in the vicinity were snuffed out instantaneously and a puff of smoke drifted towards the bishop. Jeremy turned pillarbox red and Miss Armitage was suffused with embarrassment on his behalf. 'Has anyone got a match?' hissed Jeremy, hoping that he could relight the candle without the humiliation of walking back to the vestry. None of the clergy could help him and the bishop maintained a dignified silence. Mr Crumpton felt so ashamed, and this was not helped when a box of matches was finally produced by one of the younger choirboys along with a packet of Woodbines which fell conspicuously to the floor. The bishop slid slightly to the left. The service continued, punctuated by coughs and sneezes and the occasional hiccup from Mr Newington. Mr Crumpton weakly raised himself to his feet; it took a great deal of effort as the flu had drained all his energies. He felt rather light-headed and detached. 'Let us kneel,' he croaked as his legs gave way under him. The bishop effortlessly slid off his chair on to the red velvet kneeler, whereupon a piercing pain shot through his right knee. Jeremy had left a pin in the hassock.

Old Tom snored during the bishop's address, and as he was sitting in a pew on his own that week no one could prod him awake. He always nodded off during the sermon and saw no reason why this week should be any different. When the bishop had most carefully resumed his seat, it was time for the choir to sing an anthem. In the absence of the choirmaster, Dave was in charge and so they did *not* sing an anthem. Dave produced his guitar from under a choir pew and the choir rose.

Miss Proctor played an introductory chord on the organ, then there was a pause during which Dave said 'A-one, a-two, a, one, two, three, four . . .' and the choir were let loose singing, 'If I had a hammer, I'd hammer in the morning.' As if this wasn't bad enough, the choirboys swayed to the left and right in unison clapping their hands. Mr Crumpton devoutly wished he had a hammer, because he knew what he would have done with it. Miss Proctor played a very snazzy accompaniment, but the *pièce-de-résistance* came when Jeremy produced a tambourine. Mr Crumpton sank to his knees and buried his head in his hands. Meanwhile the choir had arrived at verse two and were singing, 'If I had a bell, I'd ring it all over this land.' Miss Birch had happily lent one of her handbells for the occasion and a choirboy clanged it with enthusiasm. Miss Venables thought it was absolutely wonderful and joined in the clapping until quelled by an icy look from Miss Peebles. Actually, Miss Peebles was beginning to enjoy it but felt that congregational participation was going a little too far. Miss Dunn got up and walked out. The choir came to the last verse and sang joyfully, 'Well, I've got a hammer and I've got a bell, and I've got a song to sing all over this land. It's the hammer of justice . . .' ('Yeah!' yelled the choir) 'It's the bell of freedom. It's the song about love between all of my brothers, all – o – ver – this – land,' they finished. Jeremy shook his tambourine heartily, the bell clanged and Dave raised his hand in the air and shouted a triumphant '*Hall-e-lu-ja!*' During the ensuing stunned silence, the head dropped off the eagle.

Mr Crumpton wished he could dissolve. Even the bishop raised an eyebrow but caught himself in time and returned the solemn look to his face. The rest of the service passed in a blur for Mr Crumpton. Eventually it came to an end and he was able to retire to the vestry for a relapse. The bishop politely declined a cup of coffee and hastily packed his mitre. At the church door, Reverend Blue Jeans was promising to let Miss Venables have the music for 'If I had a hammer' and in the Lady Chapel Mr Newington was checking his reflection in the chalice. He thought he looked rather pale and wondered if an overdose of garlic could produce complications. Mr Bulmer was helping the bishop into his car when Miss Birch breezed up and said, 'Hope to see you again on Wednesday week, Bishop. Me Gel Guides are coming over for a tour of the cathedral followed by tea at the Palace.' The bishop did not look too delighted. Miss Birch slammed the car door for him and he drove off down the road with a flurry of white vestments billowing out of the car door. Lightning had struck twice; Miss Birch had repeated Jeremy's *faux pas* by trapping the bishop's robes in the door as she slammed it shut.

A week later Miss Peebles bumped into Mrs vicar in the Co-op and inquired after the vicar's health. Mrs vicar said that her husband was much recovered and that he hoped to recommence his duties in a week's time. She also added that she had heard that Mr Newington was unwell and commented how nasty the flu epidemic had been. 'Oh, he hasn't got the flu,' said Miss Peebles; 'he's in bed with nervous exhaustion.' Yes, poor Mr Newington had quite worn himself out trying to stay free of the flu. He never did locate his tonsils. Reverend Blue Jeans happily packed his guitar and returned to Mr Poddlewell's enlightened parish, leaving a dejected Mr Crumpton picking Jesus stickers off the vestry walls.

Afterword

The curate had just been lulled into the false belief that the parishioners he shepherded were becoming a passive flock when a dispute arose concerning the church garden. This occurred on the same day that Hilary Birch decided to go pot-holing under a mountain of accumulated ecclesiastical debris in the vestry. She exhumed not a body but . . . that is another story.

I can assure you that it was not long before pandemonium ensued, effortlessly generated by the irrepressible Spinsters of this Parish.